MARY LOU

Other books by John Powers

ONE GOAL
A Chronicle of the
1980 U.S. Olympic Hockey Team

YANKEES
An Illustrated History
(with George Sullivan)

THE SHORT SEASON
The Boston Celtics

MARY LOU

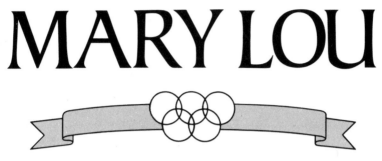

CREATING AN OLYMPIC CHAMPION

Mary Lou Retton
AND
Bela Karolyi

WITH
John Powers

McGRAW-HILL BOOK COMPANY
New York   St. Louis   San Francisco
Hamburg   Mexico   Toronto

1 2 3 4 5 6 7 8 9 D O C D O C 8 7 5

ISBN 0-07-051894-7

LIBRARY OF CONGRESS CATALOGING IN PUBLICATION DATA

Retton, Mary Lou, 1968–
    Mary Lou; creating an olympic champion.
    1. Retton, Mary Lou, 1968–   .   2. Gymnasts—
United States—Biography.   3. Karolyi, Bela.
4. Gymnastics—Coaches—Biography.   I. Karolyi, Bela.
II. Powers, John, 1948–   .   III. Title.
GV460.2.R47A35   1986   796.4'1'0924 [B]   85-12747
ISBN 0-07-051894-7

BOOK DESIGN BY KATHRYN PARISE

To my parents,
who have sacrificed a part of their lives for me.

M.L.R.

For Martha,
who has been with me in good times and bad.

B.K.

For Marie, who was a fan

J.P.

CONTENTS

ACKNOWLEDGMENTS

To Lois and Ronnie Retton, whose memories and photographs of their youngest daughter's childhood and insights about their hometown were indispensable,

To Martha Karolyi, whose recall of bygone names and places never faltered,

To John Traetta, who provided valuable editorial guidance and a wealth of resource material,

To Arthur Kaminsky, who helped shape the concept and critique the manuscript,

To Janet Pawson, whose diligence and diplomacy pulled the project together,

To Tom Quinn, who lightened daunting deadlines with aplomb and good humor,

To Judy Mayer, who kept a stream of phone numbers, clips and logistical tidbits flowing among Manhattan, Wellesley, Houston, Fairmont and Maui,

To Elaine LePage, who preserved domestic tranquility on Weston Road,

To Anne Powers, who typed the finished product with Olympian speed,

To Carla Besemann, who plucked forth results, national and international, from the U.S. Gymnastics Federation's files,

To the Marion County (West Virginia) Chamber of Commerce, which supplied vital statistics about Fairmont and environs:

We owe sincere thanks

Mary Lou Retton
Bela Karolyi,
John Powers

Mary Lou Retton, who won the all-around competition at the 1984 Olympics, was America's first gold medalist in women's gymnastics. Bela Karolyi, who left Romania in 1981 after creating a world-championship team, was her coach. This is their story.

INTRODUCTION

Not Quite a Butterfly

Eight o'clock in the evening on a winter Wednesday in Houston, with females airborne everywhere you look. Mary Lou Retton (Body by U.S. Steel) is standing in line at the head of a tumbling strip at Karolyi's Gym, preparing to launch herself ceilingward. She is wearing her working woman's clothes—black sweatshirt and leotard, with a swatch of white adhesive tape binding the top of each calf.

There is no overwhelming reason for her to be here, twisting, stretching, coaxing her sinews into peak form. Her place in gymnastics history is secure. When Mary Lou captured the all-around title with "The Vault Without Fault" at the 1984 summer Games in Los Angeles, she was the first American woman ever to win an Olympic gold medal.

But that was last year's challenge. This year's challenge is the McDonald's American Cup, which Mary Lou has won twice. No woman has ever won it three times. Enough said.

So while the floor routine that earned her a perfect 10 at the Olympics would probably suffice, Mary Lou is working on a new one, getting the choreography down, perfecting the moves. When the music and the exercise end Mary Lou is smiling into an empty corner. "Is nobody there," says her coach, Bela Karolyi, grinning.

"Okay, rotation," Karolyi calls now, nodding in the direction of the uneven parallel bars on the other side of the gym. "Rrib busterrs."

Rib busters means forty-five minutes of swinging and bumping and reaching for handholds, all of it done between five and eight feet in the air. For the Xthousandth time in her career Mary Lou tapes her wrists, chalks her hands, and gets in line. After bars she will perform six or eight routines on the balance beam, all of them observed critically by Karolyi's wife Martha, herself a former gymnast. By evening's end Mary Lou will have been in almost continuous motion for three hours.

Even if there were no competition to train for she might still have come to the gym, partly out of habit, partly because after ten years of this her body fairly screeches for a demanding workout after several days of inactivity.

Karolyi's has been Mary Lou Retton's second home ever since she arrived on the first day of 1983 from West Virginia, where she'd been the only elite gymnast in the state. At fourteen, she was already a top competitor, but she wanted to be even better. And she believed that eighteen months of intensive work with the Karolyis just might make the difference between being a United States team member and being Olympic champion.

Since then Mary Lou has spent more than three-thousand hours in this bright and airy building tucked away on a side street in a residential neighborhood twenty miles north of the city, most of them in anonymous and sweaty tedium. She may be an Olympic champion now, but at Karolyi's she is merely the next gymnast in line.

She has never felt any need to be singled out and fussed over, yet her build and her dynamism set Mary Lou apart. She is fifty-seven inches tall and most of her ninety-four pounds appear to be leg and thigh muscle. Her silhouette hardly conforms to the traditional model of a female gymnast, which is ponytailed and spindly thin. Mary Lou is constructed like a cast-iron toy truck.

After a decade of banging around hard surfaces Mary Lou's body is showing traces of wear. She has fractured a wrist, has had arthroscopic surgery on a knee, has torn the plantar fascia in a foot, and has collected an extensive assortment of bruises, and scraped and dislocated fingers. She shrugs these off as occupational hazards. Aching parts are the unavoidable fruit of gymnastics. She ices them down, tapes them up, and forgets about them.

If nothing else, Mary Lou has made toughness a virtue in women's athletics. "Of her 94 pounds," wrote one Los Angeles sports columnist during the Games, "65 are heart."

Her competitive style, based on power and speed, determination and adrenalin, optimism and grit, has changed irrevocably her sport's image. It has also made Mary Lou a role model for millions of young people, and has spurred an unprecedented gymnastics boom in the United States.

For more than a quarter of a century the sport was something of an American afterthought, its best performers only rarely contenders at the world level. In 1961, when the Soviet Union already had eight-hundred-thousand active participants and gymnastics was mandatory in school, only eleven women turned out for the U.S. national championships in the all-around. Three years later, not a single American college, school, or club had an Olympic-size (forty feet square) floor exercise mat.

Not until 1970, when Cathy Rigby won a silver on the balance beam, had an American woman earned a medal at a world championship. And until 1984 none had won an individual Olympic medal.

Prior to the seventies, gymnastics was considered not so much a sport as an art form, closer in spirit to the Bolshoi than to basketball, and its grandes dames were decidedly not teenagers. When the Soviet Union's Larissa Latynina won six medals at the Tokyo Games in 1964, she was twenty-nine years old and had two children. The women's team that represented the United States at the 1963 Pan American Games averaged twenty years of age. It was considered young.

Mary Lou Retton would not have been a gymnast in the sixties; the odds are she would have been urged toward diving. She was made for the eighties and a broader concept of what a female athlete can be. "I'm a new breed," she says, "and I think you'll see more gymnasts like me."

For generations gymnastics had been wedded to a classical, almost balletic style, with daring made subservient to grace, power secondary to elegance. The Russians and Romanians had begun changing that in the seventies, but it took a Mary Lou to create an entirely new approach to the sport, emphasizing strength, agility, and quickness. "Mary Lou," Karolyi says, "is not quite a butterfly." She is more of a bulldozer—direct, durable, relentless. Mary Lou comes from the working-class town of Fairmont in the hilly coal-mining area of northern West Virginia. To get there from Pittsburgh, the nearest large city, you take a wiggy-waggy Twin Otter commuter plane that jiggles and drops and touches down at a small regional airport at Clarksburg. Fairmont is fourteen miles to the northeast, a town of twenty-five-thousand that sits where the Tygart Valley and West Fork rivers form the Monongahela. If you set off on a raft you can drift all the way to the Mississippi and take your choice: Minneapolis or New Orleans.

Fairmont calls itself "The Friendly City," and its residents are hard-working and open. Most of them make their living directly or indirectly from the mines. Frequent hard times have made Fairmonters resilient, resourceful, and scrappy.

Mary Lou possesses all of those qualities, along with an apparently bottomless wellspring of optimism and drive. "Everything I ever did, I wanted to excel," she says. "I didn't want to go halfway on anything." That was the Retton family style. As the youngest of five, Mary Lou was eager to forge her own identity, and athletics was a natural proving ground.

Fairmont has eighteen baseball diamonds, thirty-seven outdoor basketball courts, and seven football fields, and Mary Lou cannot remember a time when she was not running loose on one of them. If girls could have played youth football, she would have been a halfback, relishing the rough-and-tumble. Instead she was lured by gymnastics and the novelty of life in midair. In seven years Mary Lou outgrew Fairmont's one program, and with the Olympics less than two years away she looked to Houston and Karolyi's high-powered training center.

Even now, with her competitive schedule scaled back and daily sessions no longer a requirement, Mary Lou still grabs her gym bag and drives over for evening workouts, knowing that her coach, who regularly puts fourteen-hundred young gymnasts through their paces, will gladly oblige her.

A three-hour workout at Karolyi's is precisely that, four 45-minute blocs of uninterrupted activity on each of the four apparatus—beam, bars, floor, and vaulting horse—that make up women's gymnastics.

The equipment has been improved and refined over the years— takeoff boards are bouncier, fiberglass has been blended with wood, floors are buttressed with springs, beams are padded. But they are no easier to deal with. The bars are set at five and eight feet, and require a woman to swing and somersault and twist above, below, and between them.

The beam is sixteen feet long, four inches wide, and four feet above the ground. A gymnast is expected to leap, flip, turn, and stretch on it as if she were frolicking along an empty sidewalk.

The vault is an interesting demonstration of practical physics, of what happens when a semiresistible force meets an immovable object. In this case a sprinting woman is flung skyward, twists and somersaults on her way down, and is supposed to land upright, like a cat dropped from a bough.

And the floor exercise is an aerobic blend of acrobatics and dance, more than a minute of unbroken movement in the air, on the floor, and in transit.

To become a world-class gymnast a woman must master each apparatus, and Karolyi has multiples of each in his twentieth-century torture chamber. Half a dozen beams are lined up in a row in the middle of the gymnasium. On one side is laid out a regulation-size floor mat. On the other, sets of bars are rigged. At either end strips for tumbling and vaulting stretch along the walls.

This is Karolyi's domain, and he sets the rules. Parents are welcome to stay and watch, but they must do so from a balcony or from benches behind a large picture window. "I don't go in their kitchen," Karolyi reasons, "and advise them what kind of soup to make for dinner."

Workouts proceed briskly and quietly with assistant coaches inspecting every move, correcting, exhorting. Girls line up to tumble, vault, swing, and leap, then line up to do it again. The only voice heard is Karolyi's guttural growl: "Fasterrr, *fasterrr*, powerrrfulll, *powerrrfulll*." The magic word is "Guuuuuud," which Karolyi utters when he sees something that satisfies him. It is spoken with discretion, but given the length of his vowels, one of his compliments lasts twice as long as anybody else's.

Karolyi runs these workouts the same way he did for nearly two decades in Transylvania, where he created from a group of kindergartners a revolutionary concept in gymnastics, and produced fourteen-year-old Nadia Comaneci, who changed the sport forever at the 1976 Olympics in Montreal.

She and her Romanian teammates, lean and fearless young teenagers, introduced a dramatic new method of performing, creating moves *between* the parallel bars, inserting twists where none was thought to be possible, and making spectacular dismounts. Traditionalists within the sport were predictably aghast. One American gymnast called the Salto Comaneci, a twisting, back-somersault dismount from the bars, "madness." But when Nadia won three gold medals at Montreal and posted not just one unprecedented perfect score of 10 but seven of them, the sport had entered the Era Comaneci.

Yet by 1984 she was twenty-two and retired, watching from the sidelines at Los Angeles, her time passed. The moves that had stunned the world were now routine, a part of any good gymnast's repertoire. What was now in vogue was Killer Gymnastics, and an American, Mary Lou Retton—bouncy, muscular, confident, uninhibited—was its foremost practitioner.

Her best events—vault and floor—were precisely those which matched her against gravity, that let her cut loose at full speed and without flight clearance. Her landing theory was uncomplicated: "You should go *blam*. So solid that you shake the arena."

Mary Lou came with unique sound effects—footsteps pounding the vault runway, the takeoff board resonating with a bang, the floor giving off an audible thud 1.4 seconds later. Her style, wrote *Boston Globe* columnist Leigh Montville, was blink . . . blink . . . BLAM.

"What's that noise out there, Martha? Sounds as if a sack of potatoes was dropped from the heavens."

"Why . . . John, come here quick. It's a little girl. A little girl has landed out here in the field."

That was exactly the sort of impact Mary Lou made on the Los Angeles Games—concussive. She came from a mountainous state where gymnastics was a rumor, had been a member of the U.S. national team for barely more than a year, and missed the 1983 world championships with an injured wrist. But by the summer of 1984 she was a thunderclap waiting for a moment. When it came, she made history—one gold medal, two silvers, and two bronzes, punctuated by perfect scores in the final two events of the all-around. "Only You, Mary Lou!" *Sports Illustrated* proclaimed on its cover.

She was the smallest American athlete at the Olympics, yet she made the largest splash. And she stamped her sport with her own revolutionary imprint. "Mary Lou is not little flower," her coach would say. "She is little flyer."

MARY LOU

MARY LOU
Fairmont Girl

The first time I really began dreaming about the Olympics was in 1976, when Nadia won her three gold medals at Montreal. I was eight years old that summer, and I can remember lying on the living room floor back home in Fairmont, watching the whole thing on television.

The Russians were really my favorites, especially Olga Korbut. She was so peppy and smiling, and I felt sorry when Nadia beat her. Still, Nadia was *so* good, and she had that instinct about her that made you root for her, too.

God, she's so lucky, I thought when I saw her on the medal stand, not knowing all the hard work that had gone into it. At that time I'd been doing gymnastics for only a year or so, pretty much for fun.

I was the youngest of five children, and all of us loved athletics. It was a natural thing in our family—we had a huge front and back yard, and a swimming pool that we used all the time. So we were brought up around sports and we just enjoyed the atmosphere, the environment.

My father was only five-seven but he'd been a great athlete himself, a guard and a sixth-man for the West Virginia basketball team. He and Jerry West captained the 1959 NCAA squad that lost by one point to California in the finals.

He was a really good baseball player, too. The Yankees signed him right out of college, and he spent five years as a shortstop in their farm system.

If my dad had been with anybody else I'm sure he would have made it to the majors. I know Detroit wanted him really badly, but New York wouldn't trade him. To this day they haven't formally released him.

It was a problem for him. Dad moved up a class every year until he reached Double A, then—boom—he couldn't go any further. Tom Tresh was always one step above him, and the Yankees already had guys like Tony Kubek and Bobby Richardson on the club.

That was the time when New York was still in the World Series every year, and the infield never changed. By 1963 he and Mom had been married for three years and already had two kids. In fact, my parents had had a baseball wedding when he was assigned to the Yankees' minor-league team in Auburn, New York.

They came out of the church under a double row of bats, and that night my mom cut the cake at home plate. They arranged their whole life around baseball, moving to a different town every spring. Each year my parents would pack up a baby crib and a high chair and a playpen and Ronnie and Shari and go to Auburn or Greensboro, North Carolina, or Augusta, Georgia, and start a new season.

Finally my dad decided he'd had enough, and went back to West Virginia and formed his own company, repairing transportation cables for the coal-mining industry. "You dummy," I used to tease him, "you could have been a big-leaguer."

All of my brothers turned out to be good baseball players, too. Ronnie played second and third base for West Virginia; Donnie is a catcher for Fairmont State; and Jerry's a shortstop for West Fairmont High. And my sister Shari was an All-American gymnast at West Virginia.

When we were growing up my mother had trouble controlling us all because there were so many of us running around screaming and yelling. Poor Mom, I'm amazed she lived through all that.

"Settle down, now," she'd keep telling us.

"Sure, Mom, sure," we'd say, and keep bouncing off the furniture.

We had a big basement downstairs with a ping-pong table, pinball and air hockey machines, a chinup bar, and all this other stuff.

There was also an old yellow couch that Shari and I used to jump from onto the floor. I'd play a lot with Jerry because he was only a year older than I was. I'd mess around with him and his friends on weekends. They'd build these little forts, these hideouts up in the woods, and they'd let me belong to their club. But I always looked up to Shari as the big sister, and wanted to do everything she did. I'd be the little brat hanging around when her friends were over, and she'd let me tag along.

I remember we'd share the bathtub, and Shari would always get in front, making me sit behind her. "Now, Mary Lou, if you want to be a cheerleader when you get big," she'd tell me, "you've got to sit in the back."

And I believed her. So I never got any hot water or any bubbles. And I'd have to rinse my hair in the dirty bathwater.

But I didn't care, not then. I thought it was neat to do what Shari did. Once I tried to teach her something, a side aerial I learned at cheerleading camp when I was around six.

"All you have to do is *this*," I said, and I turned this cartwheel without hands. So Shari tried it and broke her arm. My mom was upstairs making snickerdoodle cookies, and to this day Shari won't eat one because she associates the smell with breaking the arm.

By then my mom had already been sending us both to Monica's Dance Studio twice a week since I was four to save the lamps and chairs. It was a little place with wooden floors and mirrors and barres along the walls. We'd go after school, maybe a dozen of us, to take acrobatics, ballet, and tap.

I learned how to do the basics, like one-arm front and back walk-overs, and double splits. But there's a limit to acrobatics, and I wanted to keep going.

I don't know how my mother found out about it, but the next year we started going to West Virginia University, about twenty miles north in Morgantown, twice a week for one-hour gymnastics lessons.

The place was huge and classes were packed. There must have

been about three hundred kids there, so you only got to spend about five minutes on each event. But I still enjoyed it because I was in a gymnastics atmosphere; I was learning, and that's all I cared about.

You really couldn't get much done in that short a time but Pete Longdon, who was one of the coaches there, saw the potential in me and Shari. When I was seven he and his wife opened up a gym in Fairmont called Aerial-port, and that's how it all started.

I don't think that I or my mother ever thought about my doing gymnastics competitively at that point. But she knew I enjoyed it, and it gave us something to do, something to look forward to during the week.

Fairmont wasn't exactly a gymnastics center. It's a town of 25,000 just off Interstate 79 up in the coal-mining area not too far from Pennsylvania.

Most of the people either work in the mines or in coal-related industries, and when my great-grandfather came over from Italy, that's what he did. He worked more than sixty years in the mines, and my grandfather worked thirty-five years there.

That was before the unions. They'd be in the mines and never see daylight. They'd go in when it was dark and come out when it was dark. When my father was growing up and times were hard, the miners might only be working two or three days a week. They lived from payday to payday.

My grandfather had said he never wanted my dad to go into coal mining because he knew what he'd had to go through. My father's in the business end of it, but he still comes home dirty from work.

We weren't poor, but we weren't rich either. How the coal industry goes is how my father goes, so if the miners aren't working, he isn't either.

Every four years there was usually a strike, and they'd last three, four, five, six months with people drawing unemployment. So you had to save up for when you knew you'd be without a job, and you had to watch what you spent. So we were never extravagant; we had to work for what we wanted.

There were five of us with only seven years from oldest to youngest. Ronnie's the comedian. Shari, you know. Donnie's the middle child.

He's more quiet and serious than the rest of us, but he's got all the brains. Jerry's the most talented athlete of all of us, and I tease him about being a hot dog.

Then there's me, the errand girl. Everybody used to push me around and make me run upstairs for things. The only one I could boss around was Tarzan, our collie.

We did a lot of fun things as a family when I was young. We used to go lots of places on trips. I can remember us driving to Kennywood Park in Pittsburgh or Sea World in Ohio or Storybook Forest up in western Pennsylvania. During the summers we'd go to Rehoboth Beach in Delaware. My mom would put me in this blue leotard and send me into the ocean.

Fairmont is like a lot of places in West Virginia. Most people grow up there, marry someone from there, and stay there. Everyone's pretty much hard-working and down to earth.

The big sports are football, basketball, and baseball, and since Pittsburgh is less than a couple of hours away, people are Steeler and Pirate fans. If you're a high-school athlete the big thing is to play for WVU, the Mountaineers.

So when I began, gymnastics wasn't all that big a thing. At the start there were maybe twenty of us at Aerial-port. I'd go there on Mondays, Tuesdays, and Thursdays after supper, from six to eight, and I loved it.

Before long I was learning compulsories, and I thought that was the neatest thing. The first skill I remember doing was a roundoff back handspring back tuck. Half the big girls couldn't do that, so I was real excited. "Wow, look at me!" I said, and had everybody come over and watch.

From the beginning I never had any trouble relating to the equipment. I just got up and it felt natural. The fear factor was never there, not for me.

That's why it's so good for gymnasts to start young. The coach isn't going to have you do something where you'll hurt yourself. He'll spot you, using his hands to help you through a move or to keep you from falling. And there are pits filled with foam rubber, and mats, just to cushion you if anything happens.

When you're twelve or so and just starting out you'll look at a difficult trick and say, "I'm not doing that. No way." But when you're seven you'll do anything. If the coach tells you to jump off a bridge, you will.

That was especially true of me, because I was always the go-for-it type anyway. That was my personality; I was a daring kid. They'd tell me to do something, I'd do it. Just go and not care.

I always had that instinct in me. I was a fighter. My attitude was: I may be the youngest, but I can still do it. Being the smallest in the family, always being picked on, helped me a lot there. They used to *kill* me. So I got to be pretty much of a tomboy.

In elementary school I always wanted to play with the boys. I'd be chasing *them* around during recess, while the girls would be sitting off to the side, looking all prissy in dresses. I hated dresses.

So I really took to the gym right from the start. I loved to run and tumble and vault, and I could always do it better than almost anyone there.

I looked a little different from the other girls, but that never really bothered me. I'd heard every short joke there ever was. Our original family name was Rotundo, "round" in Italian. That told you something.

Shari was five-two and she had some length to her, but I realized pretty early what my build was going to be. I was skinny at first— my mom said that when I was born all she saw was these long dark eyelashes. But I just looked at my father and my brothers and saw how my thighs and calf muscles were growing, and I just knew. "Mary Lou," I told myself, "you're not going to have long legs."

Mom called me Miss Flexibility because I didn't have any. So I knew I wouldn't look graceful in floor exercise, doing these pique turns and ballerina moves. It just wasn't my body type. But I was a good sprinter, and I had a lot of power and explosiveness, so I could do things that some of the other girls couldn't.

In workouts sometimes we'd match skills on different events. "If you give me a double back," one of the other gymnasts might say to me, "I'll give you a trick on beam."

I hated the beam. I knew from the beginning my build wasn't right

6

for it. My feet were small—would you believe size three?—and they turned in. It's much better to have big feet which turn out. And I had trouble stretching my body, which was always tight, the way you have to stretch it to look good up there.

But vaulting and tumbling just came naturally to me, and after I'd been working out at Aerial-port for a while, things just began getting better and better.

I remember going to my first competition at Parkersburg, a town on the Ohio border, when I was about eight. I had this blue and white tie-dyed leotard with three little red stars at the bottom. I thought it was my U.S.A. uniform.

I got a 1 on bars and thought it was a 10. This was after the 1976 Olympics where Nadia had gotten the first 10 in gymnastics history. But the scoreboard couldn't go that high, so they put up a 1.

Well, I had a couple of falls. Pete was spotting me all the way through the routine, and every time your coach touches you, it's a point off your score.

So they put up the 1 and I was thrilled. "I got a ten, I got a ten," I went around telling everyone. I forgot who broke it to me that I didn't.

Later I went to the West Virginia state meet and won the Class III title, which was for beginners. That was a big deal for me, but I don't even think I was nervous. I just kind of went and did my thing.

I don't even think I knew what I was getting myself into. My mom and I certainly never had any serious ideas about my being world-class. Not then, anyway.

The big gymnastics competitions, like Championships of the U.S.A. and Worlds, weren't shown on television that often. But when they were, I was glued to the set. Just watching them would get me determined.

"I'm gonna go in the gym tomorrow," I'd tell myself, "and really work hard." That's why Nadia really inspired me. I'd seen those tricks before, but I'd never seen them done perfectly the way she'd done them.

I knew she was ahead of me by a lot. I mean, at that time I was only spending a half a dozen hours a week in the gym. So I knew I

7

had to work my butt off, but I was ready for that. I had no idea how good I'd ever be, but I still had my dream.

"Mary Lou," I'd tell myself, "you're going to be in the 1984 Olympics." I had it timed out perfectly in my head, even at that age. I'd be sixteen years old that summer, and I'd be at my prime. So it was always 1984 for me. Always.

MARY LOU
Making the Choice

You always dream about the Olympic Games, but Nadia and I and every gymnast had to start the same way—learning the skills on every apparatus. Everyone has their favorite, the one they're best on, but they usually have to work like horses to get the other ones up to par.

I had no problem with vaults or tumbling, because they're suited to my natural abilities, my speed and explosiveness. Bars I enjoyed because you could swing.

But the beam wasn't fun at all. It wasn't fast, and my flexibility was *so* bad. I'd have to get up there and do splits, and I just couldn't. Or didn't want to. It took me a while to understand you really did have to do all four events and that each one demands a special approach.

Beam is the hardest because it's only four inches wide, and that limits you. And because it's four feet off the ground there's a little bit of a fear factor, too.

That's why they usually start beginners by putting the beam on the floor and holding their hands while they walk across it and get the feel. It takes a couple of days just to feel comfortable up there.

After a while they raise the beam a little bit off the floor, then midway, then to full height, using floor mats as a cushion. Finally they take the mats away, and you're on your own.

It's scary and complicated at first, but the coach spots you. You put your hands down and feel the beam the whole way. You start with simple things like forward rolls, then you progress to tougher skills like cartwheels and roundoff moves.

Some people, like Tracee Talavera and Ecaterina Szabo, are made for the beam. I'm not. My personality is exactly opposite what you need up there. Patience is a virtue, and you need patience on beam. If you don't keep your concentration all the way to the end, you can fall. And if you mess up a beam, it's a *major* fall. If you slip during a floor routine you can always make a little pose out of it and cover it up. If you fall on a beam routine it's four feet to the floor and everybody sees it.

It's really tough if you fall at the beginning, because you've still got the rest of the routine to go, and there are lots of places where you can fall again. You just have to tell yourself, "Okay, it's over," and put it out of your mind.

That's why it's important to get a good, solid mount. If you get on and your hips are crooked and your feet aren't in the middle, it's going to throw the whole pass off.

A lot of people try a difficult mount because they figure it's a good way to pile up points. Sure, it's spectacular, and they probably get the credit they want from the judges. But I think it's better to get up on the beam clean, then end with a hard dismount.

Bars can be a problem for young girls just starting out because your hands are smaller and they don't fit around as well. As you get older you grow into the apparatus, but bars is the most difficult event to make changes in.

It's a matter of habit and rhythm and direction. Your mind is saying, "Wait. We've got to go *this* way now. We're trying something new."

So it takes a while, and sometimes you do wind up falling and bruising your shin or getting a scratch somewhere because you're going against your body. You want to turn a different way, and your body's saying, "No, no, you're not supposed to do this."

It can be a little scary learning a new trick on bars. The first few times everything's so new you don't have any sense of where you are. You're eight feet off the ground on the high bar, and if you're in the middle of a routine and feel yourself falling, you see the low bar coming and you're worrying whether you're going to crack your head.

Falling on bars is even worse than beam because it breaks everything up. You're already tired, and you have to chalk up and get back up again and finish. Falling takes it all out of you.

The biggest thing to remember is to take your time. That's one thing I learned from Julianne McNamara. I used to be real quick on bars, thinking I had to rush through it. But you have more time up there than you think. You want to long it out, get full extension on handstands. With my body type I really had to pay attention to that. A long-limbed girl like Julianne looks very nice on bars. Me, no. So I've learned to slow it down, to stretch it out, point my toes, and go for amplitude.

The vault is difficult, too, because you've got so many things to think about, and it's so quick, only a matter of seconds. You have to worry about the run, hitting the board, placing the hands on the horse, doing your moves in the air, and landing solid, sticking it.

It can be frightening running full speed, knowing that if you mess up you're going crashing into the horse. So I can see where people get intimidated by it. But you still have to go full out because speed is the key. You're going horizontal and suddenly you have to punch it and go vertical, so you need all the momentum you can get. That's why when you see some girl trotting down there, you almost want to shout, "Run. Would you *run?*"

I always start my run in the same spot—73.5 feet back. I always take the same number of steps, and always hit the board in the same place. If you take a longer or a shorter step somewhere, it screws everything up. When I do that, I don't even bother going over. I just veer off to the side. That's how much the run means.

Placing the hands is important, too. If they're a little off you can still have a decent vault, as long as both hands are on the front side. But if you have one in the wrong place or one slips, it's going to throw you off.

You have to hit the whole sequence right or the vault won't come off. That's why you have to prepare your mind early so you know what's coming up and your body just does it.

Floor exercise is where you've got more room to experiment, which is probably why that event has changed so much over the last ten years. At the Montreal Olympics Nadia was doing double fulls and that was considered daring. Double fulls are nothing now. Floor used to be a lot of graceful dance steps and turns and some easy tumbling. These days the tumbling is much harder, and you're going to see even more of that. No one's looking for the dance anymore. If they wanted to see dancing, they'd go to the ballet.

The crowd is there to see activity gymnastics, and great tumbling is impressive to them. All of that helped me, because with my body type I couldn't go out there and try to be a ballerina. I have to do something dynamic with a lot of sharps and poses to it because that's the way I move.

For a long time that was a big conflict. "Oh, she moves like a robot," people would say. "She can't dance." What can you do? I couldn't do it, not in the graceful style people had gotten used to. It was very frustrating. It used to kill me, and I'd cry sometimes. "Why me?" I'd ask myself. "I can't be what they want me to be." But there was nothing I could do about it. I just didn't fit the classical mold. I was short and muscular and a good all-around athlete.

Until I was in the sixth grade gymnastics was just something I enjoyed doing. It was a priority, of course, but it wasn't serious-serious. There were lots of other things I enjoyed doing, too. I was a Pop Warner majorette one year, a Pee Wee cheerleader another. I was even Pee Wee homecoming queen.

And I still did a lot of other sports, most of them with boys. During recess in elementary school I'd race them and play whiffleball. The other girls would play a little, but they weren't really into it. I was *really* into it. I always wanted to pitch. I was practically brought up on a baseball diamond and a football field.

I was always a pretty good sprinter. I could beat a lot of the boys— they didn't like that at all—and when I was eleven I went to the nationals in the Hershey's track and field competition and finished second in the fifty-yard dash. I'd never run in a real race or anything, but I was ahead right until the end when some girl with long legs beat me by a step.

But by the time I was twelve, I began getting serious about gymnastics. I'd done well enough in Class III that I skipped intermediates and went straight to Class I, and I'd gotten more mature and stopped goofing around in workouts.

Gary Rafaloski, who'd taken over as coach at Aerial-port when Pete Longdon left to coach college girls in New Mexico, started giving me longer workouts with more discipline. That was when I began thinking maybe I can do this fairly well. What it meant, though, was forcing myself to be a lot more dedicated. When you decide you want to be national caliber, workouts have to become habit. You need that drive inside of you that says: "Go to the gym."

You have to make yourself show up there on a regular basis and train despite the aches and injuries. Just being in the gym day after day, jumping and stretching and landing on hard surfaces and banging off wooden equipment, makes for a lot of wear and tear on your body.

The beam is hard on your feet because of all the pounding. You develop blood blisters from bouncing on your big toe all the time. You get bruises on the balls of your feet and on your heels because you have to land so hard and solid, and the beam's really not that padded. And the padding is leather, like rawhide, so you get rug burns from scraping against it.

On bars you're always ripping your hands and building up callus from all the twisting and the friction. I had to put Vaseline and vitamin E on them and wear tube socks with holes cut out at night. You catch your fingers on the bars, bend them back, break them, and dislocate them so you have to pull them out.

If you belly-beat the low bar the way I do, you get big bruises on your hips. You're coming from a handstand and you have all that momentum building on your way down. The bar gives a little bit, but it's still wood or fiberglass and it's still hard. You can put in pads called "belly-bumpers" to protect your hips during workouts, but you can't use them in competition. And if you're off-center you can bang up your ribs so badly that it hurts to breathe.

That happens every day. You turn ankles and sprain wrists and pull muscles. Sometimes I'd wake up with fresh bruises here and there, and wonder how I got them.

All you could do when you got home was draw a hot bath and just lie in it and relax until the soreness began to go away. I'd be in there so long that my mom would come in and check on me. "You still there?" she'd ask me. But the longer I stayed at it, the more I could see myself improving.

When I was twelve I went to the Class I nationals in Tulsa, which was really scary for me. All these girls from all over the United States were there, girls I'd read about in *International Gymnast.* Oh, my God, that girl was in the magazine, I'd think. And she's *here.* What am I doing here?

It was stunning. I was awed. But somehow I won the vault, was second on floor, and finished seventh in the all-around. My next goal was junior elite, and that was a huge step. All of the girls at that level were the ones who'd been getting their pictures in *International Gymnast,* and all of them were serious-serious about the sport.

At that point I had to make the decision—am I going to go all out for it, or am I not going to do it at all? Because if I wasn't going to fully dedicate myself, it wouldn't be worth it. It becomes a question of what you're shooting for. What are you in that gym to prove? Do you want to make the junior national team? The senior team? Go to the world championships? The Olympics?

Everybody at that level, especially the eastern Europeans and the Asians, is a full-time gymnast. The Russians and East Germans and Romanians have been in special schools since they were in kindergarten. If you're even going to compete against them, much less beat them, you have to train with the same intensity they do.

Anybody with talent faces that dilemma around twelve or thirteen, when it comes time to think about junior elite. Make the choice—school activities or gymnastics—knowing that if it's gymnastics, your whole life is going to change.

It's tough, especially in this country, because of the peer pressure. Your friends are always going off to dances or movies or Friday night basketball games. "You coming with us?" they ask you. "No? Then we don't want you in our crowd."

A lot of gymnasts can't do that, they can't handle it. So they quit.

I know several girls who were elite gymnasts, potential Olympians, who just decided that they didn't want to sacrifice that much.

But at that point I knew what I wanted to do. I figured I could always make up for lost time in college. But my schedule then just wouldn't allow for both.

After a while I was doing special workouts with Gary in the afternoons, so that limited what I could do after school. I also had evening workouts, so that ruled out Fridays. When I had competitions they were on weekends, and more often than not you'd have to travel to them.

So I missed the high-school football games, the dances, the usual teenage stuff. I never dated, really. At times it was lonely. You'd go to school the next day and everyone would be talking about the game the night before and how good it was. And you're just kind of sitting there feeling left out.

In seventh and eighth grade, that's when you really want to be a schoolgirl. Oooh, I want to go to basketball games, too, I'd think, but I've got workout. But at the same time, I knew once I made junior elite I could start traveling and seeing different things, and that was really neat. If you made the junior national team they'd send you all over the world for competitions, and I'd barely been out of West Virginia.

I'd had a taste of that when I went up to Washington for the Capital Cup, which had all the big East Coast clubs like the Parkettes, the MGs, and the Marvateens competing. That was the first time a lot of people saw me, the first time other coaches started noticing. I got my name on the front page of the *Washington Post* sports section, which I thought was a real big deal.

Well, I made the junior national team, and when I was thirteen I went up to Canada for my first international with Dianne Durham and some girls from the East. I had to go down to the post office and get a passport application. Hey, I'm important now, I thought. I've got a passport.

I also had a concussion, which I got from messing up a double back the week before, and banging my head against a wall. But I still

won the all-around at the competition, which was a dual meet between the United States and Canada, and that's when things began
happening for me.

I never even got to go home. When I got off the plane in Pittsburgh,
they were paging me. It was the U.S. Olympic Committee and they
wanted me to get right on another plane and go to Syracuse for the
National Sports Festival, which is an annual competition for potential
Olympians.

That was my first time on national television, and everyone back
home went wild—"Hey, Mary Lou's on TV!" I sprained my wrist
and finished second behind Beth Pope, who eventually became one
of my teammates in Houston.

But Sugar Ray Leonard signed my splint, and when I got home
there was an autographed picture from Larry Holmes congratulating
me for winning in Canada. I'd never even met him.

That was the beginning of a lot of trips for me, and while it was
exciting, it was also lonely at times. I remember leaving for a big
meet once, and when my mom picked me up at school to take me
to the airport I cried because I was missing the Christmas party.

Once she took a picture of me with my bags packed, and you
should see my face. I really didn't look like I wanted to go. Mom
would get all nervous, too, at the idea of me going off by myself.
She'd wait until she thought the plane had landed, then she'd call
the airport to make sure it had.

When I was fourteen, I went to Hamamatsu for a dual meet with
Japan, which was a really big thing for me. I flew by myself to Los
Angeles, met the rest of the American team, and flew eleven hours
across the Pacific on JAL. I remember they were serving us Japanese
food and, like typical American teenagers, we all scrunched up our
faces and went "Eeeewww." But we were all hyped up, running up
and down the aisles.

Japan was so different from anything I'd ever experienced. Competing overseas is always a big adjustment. It's not just the food and
the language and the customs. The equipment is really different and
the spectators are, too.

In the States if you have a fall everybody goes "oooohhh." In Japan they giggle—hee-hee-hee. I did fall, on beam, and everybody did go hee-hee-hee.

The next summer, in 1982, they took us to Peking for a meet with China, which was the first time I had real Chinese food. I prefer the American kind.

I went everywhere that year—to Asia, to South Africa, to Los Angeles, to Fort Worth, to Philadelphia, to Salt Lake City, to Reno. So it didn't bother me that much that I was missing out on school activities.

I was at Fairmont Catholic then, and the people there were great about letting me take time off for competitions. I'd take my books with me, and they'd give me work to do, so I didn't have any school problems.

Anyway, I was learning about a lot of things they don't teach in school. When all my friends were reading about the Great Wall of China, I was walking on it. Coming back to Fairmont and telling everybody about it, that made it all worthwhile.

I was traveling and I was improving. I was up there with Dianne Durham and all the other top gymnasts my age, and the Olympics was only two years away.

But the whole time the Games were getting closer, I was getting restless. I could see other girls from other gyms getting better, making more progress than I was. I was the only elite gymnast in the whole state, and I'd run out of people who could push me the way I needed to be pushed. I could see I had to make a change, even if it meant leaving home.

3

MARY LOU
The Right Thing, the Right Time

Nobody likes to leave home for a long period of time, especially when you're a teenager. Everything you've ever known is there—your family, your friends, your school, all the places you hang around. And I love Fairmont, I really do. I spent my whole life growing up there, and the people were always great, supporting me in everything I ever tried.

When I'd begun competing seriously, a man named Baker Nicholson, who owned three McDonald's restaurants in the area, formed a booster group that raised a lot of money to help pay my expenses. I couldn't have made it without them.

But by the end of 1982 I knew in my heart I had to leave there if I wanted to become the best gymnast I could. I'd been thinking about it for a year by then and mentioning the idea to my parents.

I'd been going to these national events with other junior elites, and I'd begun noticing that all these girls I'd competed against in Class I were improving. And I wasn't. It wasn't that I wasn't doing well. I mean, I was placing in the top five, but I wasn't getting any better.

Everyone says, well, when you're at that level you should push yourself. Well, sure you push yourself, but it's not the same. I was working out five days a week in Fairmont, two hours a day. But that was it.

Most of the time I was in the gym myself, doing private one-to-one workouts with Gary Rafaloski, and there just wasn't enough intensity in them. I would do one bar routine, and if I made it, it was all right, it was let's go on to the next event. So workouts were a breeze. I got away with murder, but secretly I wanted to be pushed, to have someone yell at me if I needed it. That just wasn't Gary's style. He was more the quiet type.

So I was pretty much on my own in the gym and on the road whenever I went to major competitions, I'd be the only one in that style of leotard. I had no teammates from my own club to hang out with, and it was kind of sad and boring. I'd be in a hotel room all by myself, and I'd hear girls from some other club yelling and having fun next door. Then, when I went into competition, I'd be by myself in a group. I really felt lonely.

"Oh," I'd hear people say, "she's the little girl from West Virginia." I just felt really intimidated, and didn't like it at all.

But coming back to my own gym in Fairmont was even worse. That was always the depression time for me. The other gymnasts were all going back to where there were girls at their own level, and I'd be coming back to the same old stuff, the one-to-ones, the routines. I never could develop that attitude of "Gosh, I've got to do better than *her*." And that competitiveness is needed to improve.

That's when I'd start talking to my parents about leaving. "Look," I'd tell them. "I was doing good and having fun with the girls at the competition and then I come back and there's nothing for me here. I don't want to *do* this any more."

"Oh, it's okay," they'd tell me. "You're doing fine." I think deep down they knew I had to make a change, too, but they didn't want to admit it.

But as the months went on it became obvious that something had to happen. I'd come home from workouts sometimes so frustrated that I'd begin to cry. "I want to go," I'd say. "I want to move away. I want to get the right training."

Other people had been telling me that for a while. "The coaches have been talking about you," they'd say. "They think you could go a long way."

Maybe you have to be in gymnastics to understand what a big

19

thing it is to improve your routines by even a tenth of a point. There's such a major difference between a 9.8 and a 9.9, and it all has to do with how technically clean you are. You get higher scores for trying more difficult skills, but it's also a question of how well you can execute them. It doesn't make much sense to do a layout Tsukahara vault or a Comaneci dismount from the bars if your legs are apart or you can't stick the landing. Every little mistake—a wobble on the beam, a hop on a landing, a slipped hand on the bars—can cost you a tenth of a point, and in our sport, that's the difference between first and second.

I knew, just from how I did my own routines and from having watched other girls doing theirs, that I wasn't as clean as I could be. There are lots of little things that only a gymnast or a judge or a coach notices, but they're big things when you're competing at the national or world level.

I was still a junior then, but I knew that in 1983 I'd be competing as a senior against a lot of gymnasts who'd made Olympic teams and been to world championships. If I stayed in Fairmont maybe I'd still make the Olympic team, or at least be an alternate. But to be a serious medal contender I'd have to eliminate those little flaws, to sharpen my routines, and add new and more difficult skills.

I needed someone pushing and pushing me, and I needed some other girls around me who were shooting for the same thing I was. So I decided I had to make the move. I knew I was ready for it. I just wasn't sure where to go or what to do. The nearest big program was the Parkettes, up in Allentown, Pennsylvania. There was the National Academy of Artistic Gymnastics in Oregon, and SCATS— the Southern California Acro Team—in Huntington Beach. And then there was Karolyi's in Houston.

I didn't know Bela at all, but I'd seen his girls and I was impressed. They were so ready and so confident, and Bela was always beside them, getting them hyped up. You get thirty seconds in warmups, but instead of what most gymnasts do, just going through parts and not really caring, Bela's girls would do a full routine—boom, stick. As soon as one was done, he'd be setting the bars for another. And he had them so mentally prepared that they had no doubts.

Of course, I'd heard all these terrible rumors about Bela—he's this monster, he starves you, he makes you into a robot. So I began asking other gymnasts, like Dianne Durham, "How *is* Bela? Is he nice?"

"Oh," Dianne shrugged, "he's just like any other coach." So I really had no idea. Finally, in the summer of 1982 at the junior nationals in Salt Lake City, I went up and talked to him.

He was in the hospitality room eating, and I went in to get a drink. "Oh, hi Bela," I said, and we began to chat. He told me a little about his gym, then he wrote down his name and number.

"Call me," he said. "I want you to come down and try it out."

"Sure," I said. I was so excited, because by then I was definitely looking around. When I left the room I ran up to my parents.

"Mom, look," I said, and showed her the name and number. She was a little skeptical. "He just wants you to go down there," she said.

Well, I was upset. "You know," I said, "this man knows what he's doing." I'd seen his girls perform, and I'd seen how he urged them on and pushed them. His personality was a big part of it, too. We were so much alike, so open and hey-how-you-doing? And knowing he'd been Nadia Comaneci's coach convinced me even more. So my mind was set.

The next time we saw him was two days before Christmas at a meet in Reno, Nevada. By this time it was clear to my parents that I really wanted to get away. My dad understood because he'd been an athlete and he knew that coaching was so important.

Now, my dad went up to Bela. "What do you think about my daughter?" he asked him.

"She has the natural ability," Bela said, "but the time before the Olympics is so short. She would have to come down right now in order to do it."

Everything happened so quickly after that, I still can't believe it. We had a big family discussion about it when I got home. Was I mature enough to handle the responsibility of being away on my own? Would I be able to manage my money and do my schoolwork and deal with being homesick?

Who knows those answers for sure when you're only fourteen? But I thought I could. My parents left the decision up to me. "We're not pushing you into it," they said, "but if you think you want to do it. . . ."

There was no question in my mind that I wanted to. I realized what the consequences were, having to leave my family and live with different people in a strange city under a new coach. But that's what I'd wanted for a year.

My mom didn't really want to see her baby leave, but she was willing to let me go. It was going to cost them thousands and thousands of dollars a year, but I don't think that made any difference to my parents. They were willing to make the financial sacrifice, as long as I was sure it was what I wanted.

I knew my moving away would be hard for us all, but I was excited because I knew I was doing the right thing. I knew I was going to the right coach and the right team at the right time. And I knew that if I didn't go, I'd never really know whether I could have made it to the Olympics. For the rest of my life I would have thought, well, I could have made it if . . . . There always would have been that *if*.

The only thing left was to break the news to Gary, and that was the hardest thing ever. So the day after Christmas my dad went down to Aerial-port and told Gary that I was leaving and going to Houston to Karolyi's.

Well, Gary was shocked—and mad. I don't think he had any idea this would happen. "I don't believe this," he said, "I can take her to the Olympics."

"Well, she's been at the same point for a year now and she's not improving," my dad told him. "And Bela thinks she can do it."

Gary was angry at Bela, because he thought Bela was recruiting me. It was hard for him, because Gary thought he was doing his best, and he was. But he couldn't take me any further.

"We're not saying you're a bad coach," my father told him. "But Mary Lou needs to be with girls at her own level." I think that Gary realizes all that now, but I knew he was very hurt then and I felt badly about it.

But I wanted someone to push me, even yell at me—*do* it, *do* it!— and I wasn't getting that. What I needed even more were girls like

Dianne around who'd be neck and neck with me every day, day after day, forcing me to get better.

Well, there were different reactions in Fairmont when I decided to go to Houston. Some people called up saying, "Don't do it, don't do it." And my parents got some flak from people who thought we felt I was too good for the town and that's why I was going away. I can understand why they might feel that way. Some people in other states look down on West Virginia because they think we're twenty-five years behind the times. Folks back home are sensitive about that, because they're hard-working and have a lot of pride.

So that's the reason why most people in the town, especially those who knew me or knew about athletics, were all for me going to Houston if that's what I felt I had to do. "You can put Fairmont on the map," they told me. They wanted me to make it real big.

So there was no question—I was leaving. And on Thursday, two days before the New Year, my parents and I drove off to Texas. It was such a strange feeling. I'd been telling my friends for two years that I'd be going away, that I had to, and they'd said, "Sure, sure."

Well, the night before I left I went to my brother's high school basketball game and my friends realized that it was finally happening. They were all crying, and I was crying, too. "I'll be back in two years," I kept telling them. "Don't change."

That was what everybody thought, including my parents. "You'll go to Houston," my mom always said. "You'll be down there for two years or whatever, you'll train, you'll go to the Olympics. And whatever happens, you'll come home and go back to high school here in Fairmont." And that's what I was thinking the whole time, too. Ohh, did I have another think coming to me.

The day we left my dad had borrowed the neighbor's station wagon to fit all my stuff in, all my clothes, my jewelry, my good-luck stuffed animal. . . .

It was exciting, but a little bit scary, like going off to see the Wizard of Oz. I had my birth certificate, my passport, my insurance papers. But I didn't know what to expect. I didn't know what Bela would be like. He'd told me he had a very nice family for me to live with, but

I hadn't met them. I didn't know who they were. So I really had mixed feelings about it all. We passed the West Virginia state borderline, and I continued to look back over my shoulder.

It was a two-day drive, and the whole way my parents and I kept convincing each other that this was a good thing. "Oh, yeah it really is. You're ready. Look at Nadia. He *has* to be a good coach. It's only a couple of years." All that stuff you tell yourself when you're not sure what you're getting into.

We arrived in Houston on New Year's Day, and went to the Spillers' house, the family I'd be living with. Their daughter Paige was a year younger than me, and she was one of Bela's better gymnasts. It turned out that it was their turn to host the annual New Year's party for the neighborhood, so everybody on Baltic Street was there and I got to meet them all right away.

And the very next day I was in the gym with Dianne Durham, a couple of other elite girls, and a coach I couldn't understand. Except for one word—no. No, no, no, he'd say, shaking his head when I'd finish a routine. I heard that word a lot that first day, and for a long time afterward.

Mary Lou (right) as a toddler, with cousin Rhea Larry.

A six-year-old ballerina, direct from Monica's Dance Studio.

Mary Lou at three— a rare formal portrait.

Nine years old, a Pop Warner cheerleader.

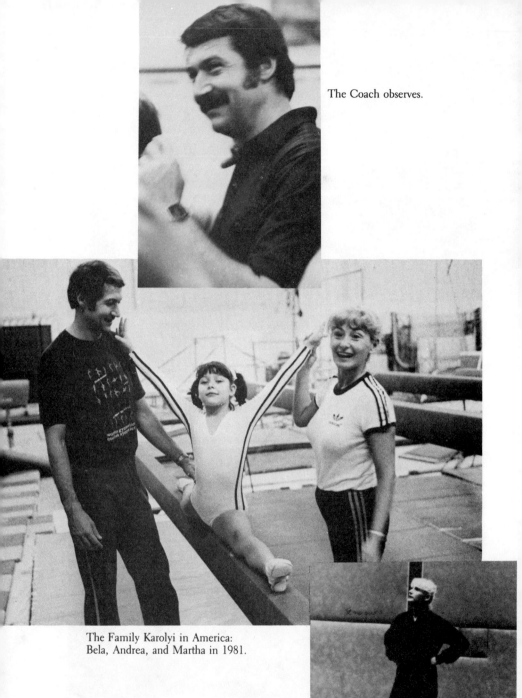

The Coach observes.

The Family Karolyi in America:
Bela, Andrea, and Martha in 1981.

Martha Karolyi, hawk-eyed
inspector of routines.

Bela figuring the odds.

Mary Lou and Bela in 1984.

Bela spots Mary Lou on
the vault.

© Dave Black, 1985

(*Above*) Mary Lou on the beam and on the money at Los Angeles.

(*Right*) The Beam—a gymnast is expected to leap, flip, turn, and stretch upon it as if she were frolicking along an empty sidewalk.

Mary Lou's perfect floor exercise in the all-around final: "She grinned and spun and went up on tiptoe, bounced and flexed and grinned again."

Mary Lou on the bars at Los Angeles: "Control yourself up there," she thought.

© Dave Black, 1985

The Retton Flip, designed to leave her sitting on the high bar in a look-ma-no-hands pose.

© Dave Black, 1985

Mary Lou's all-around beam routine: "Patience is a virtue, and
you need patience on beam."

Mary Lou on beam at Los Angeles, midway through the routine of a lifetime.

© Dave Black, 1985

The "Vault Without Fault"

"Mary Lou didn't need to look over at the judges or wait for their score. Perfect. Both her arms went up, like a referee signaling a touchdown."

Andy Hayt/SPORTS ILLUSTRATED

Mary Lou on the medal stand: "This is the moment I worked nine years for."

Andy Hayt/SPORTS ILLUSTRATED

The gold-medal press conference: "Nobody thought it could be done. But you know what? I went and did it!"

4

BELA

The Romanian Miracle

What they call the Romanian miracle began in 1963 in a small coal-mining town in Transylvania. My wife Martha and I had just graduated from the physical education institute in Bucharest and were looking for two jobs together. But the only possibility in the whole country was to go back somewhere up in the north and work in a little village.

I had grown up in that area, and my grandfather had been the first teacher in that town, which was called Vulcan. He had put together a singing and acting group and, later, an opera. He had always been doing something culturally for the miners. So I called some people there.

"Hey," I said, "do you need a physical education teacher?"

"Well," they tell me, "there is a school around here and we may have an opening." The mayor there was a simple miner but a very bright, honest, strong-working person. "Bela," he tells me, "come back to your roots and try to do something for our kids."

Now, you know the custom of miners in that area. They come out after ten or fifteen hours of work, and they are going directly to the restaurant to get a schnapps. They are drinking until they cannot walk, and the wives are coming with the wheelbarrow and putting the men in, with the children holding their hands, and are carrying them home.

This happens every single payday, and you can understand because the miner never knows if he will be coming out of that hole or not. They were dying, sometimes 150 and 200 at a time, and it was no big deal. The explosions and gas burnings, getting buried—that was the miner life, and it was nothing strange to me because I grew up there. So I decide, sure, I want to go back. And I took the position in that town, and Martha took one in another village close by. That was how we start.

I walked in the first day and these little miner kids are standing there in street clothes and big boots. They've never taken physical education and don't know what it means. I try to line them up, and there is no way. I have to go step by step.

The first time I suggested that they take off their clothes and be in T-shirts and shorts, it was like a revolution. It was unheard of. Those mothers, they almost bit me. "What the hell is going on with that corruption?" they say. "My child will never take off her clothes." I try to explain, but there is no chance. "You don't explain to me nothing," the mothers tell me. "This is bad morality."

It becomes clear to me that I have to do everything personally. So I come one day in T-shirt and shorts, and everyone is looking. The next day, is not so curious. "See, is better," I tell the kids. "Doesn't tear up your pants." Well, in a few weeks, one of the bigger boys shows up in a T-shirt. Then another boy. Then the rest. With the girls we had a bigger problem. It took a longer time. But gradually we are accomplishing something, and it was a big satisfaction.

Everybody was so excited and so positive, because they never experience anything like it. The mayor came often and watched, because he was so pleased at little miner kids doing something healthy.

I organize competitions in soccer and track and field and cross country, and the parents become interested and the whole town gets behind us. The kids, they are just eating me up, following blindly. If I say 2 o'clock in the night we are climbing Mount Everest, they are ready to do it.

If they wanted to pick the cornfields and needed help from the children, they would say, "Ask Bela." In Romania it is bad weather in the fall—rain, mud, miserable. Nobody wanted to go. But I say, let's pick that corn, and everybody does. There is a feeling of pride now, to belong to the team.

So we had a pretty good program for the older children, but what was bothering me was the situation for the young ones. Over there the schools are different. The elementary schools, which have grades one through four, are totally separated from grades five through twelve. They are not even in the same building. The little-bitty ones, they did absolutely nothing. They could not run for the soccer ball, and they didn't like it. I gave them a basketball, they couldn't hold it. What to do? Then I remembered—my true love was hiding in gymnastics.

I had been a good athlete in school. I set several national records in the hammer throw, played for Romania's team handball squad that won the world championship, and did some boxing. But when I went to college I couldn't pass the practical physical examination in gymnastics, which was a requirement to graduate from the physical education institute. It was disappointing, surprising, embarrassing. I am large, heavy, strong, but big dummy. I couldn't turn upside down on the rings. The blood would come into my head, I couldn't breathe. So I realize how little I can handle my own body, how little I know about my personal abilities.

At the same time I was watching the advanced guys on the college team, and they were so confident, so exact, so correct, specific, controlled, organized. I admired how fresh and clean they were. Like roosters, all the time ready to bite and to respond to you, but excellent people and fine students, the best in our institute. I would watch them, my eyes going back and forth, and I saw Martha there, who was one of the good gymnasts. She was amazing to me, what she could do. To see somebody bending and having so much flexibility, doing back handsprings and walkovers on the beam. I couldn't believe somebody could do it.

So one day, when nobody was there, I tried to get up on that beam. Like a monkey I am holding with my arms and my legs, and I couldn't do it. My God, I think, how can these people flip on this thing? All these things were new impressions and new sensations to me. Now, I was supposedly too old, too tall, too heavy to do anything

27

in gymnastics, but the challenge is an attraction to me. So I start intensively every morning, and I begin to feel my body, to feel the movements. And every day I make a little progress. It was motivating, to see how far I can go.

In time I get stronger and more coordinated, and by the end of the year I catch up to everybody in my group. I keep going, and in the second year gymnastics becomes an obsession. In the third year I make the college team. To do that, even as sixth person, was more of an achievement to me than winning the national hammer title. It was for me more than just a sport, it was a contest of wills, a rewarding process of building a stronger personality.

So now in our little coal-mining town we decide to teach gymnastics to the little ones, and they love it right away. In three months they learned so much. Martha and I were thrilled. Before long we put on an exhibition. It was just some tumbling, with a mini-trampoline, but the miners couldn't believe it. They said it was the biggest miracle in their lives. They were looking with tears in their eyes at their children, these little bugs flipping and doing cartwheels, standing in nice position and marching gymnastically. And we begin to get some support.

The parents couldn't do anything themselves. They were poor people, and I could never ask them for any kind of material contribution. But the town started to raise some money, and I bought some equipment, and we made the rest. The carpenters were cutting the wood for a horse and a few beams and even a couple of uneven bars. So we set up a pretty nice little gymnasium, and the kids, they progress very well.

What fantastic determination, what tremendous physical potential, what mental drive these youngsters naturally they have! It is such a pleasure to work with them. They are sucking everything from you, and they are so pleased with everything you are doing for them. They are excited, we are excited, and their accomplishments are unbelievable. So during the second year we went out to compete in a zone meet, where several towns are getting together.

At that time girls would get involved in gymnastics at fifteen or sixteen, the boys at eighteen or nineteen. Well, we show up with these tiny seven-, eight-, nine-year-olds to compete with young ladies, women, all over sixteen. You can imagine the reaction. They couldn't disqualify us, because there was no age limit. But at the same time, nobody wanted to give us the recognition for winning. It was huge dilemma for them. Nobody wanted to have the little ones beating the big ones.

So finally the officials compromised. "This experimental team from Vulcan, they performed very well in exhibition," they announced. "Let's give them a big trophy and have them go home. And the winners are. . . ." They light up the winners' names, and it is a high-school team from one of the biggest towns there.

So we went home and we were happy, but we were hurt. It wasn't right and it wasn't fair, because we had beaten very badly the first-place team.

Anyway, our appearance there provoked a big discussion with very different reactions. "Great," some people said. "Look at these guys, what they did." "Oh, those criminals," others said. "Crippling the kids. Can you imagine what will happen to them after a year? Those children will be physical wrecks. The Karolyis are breaking their bones. They'll be bent and crooked and hunchbacked. This has to be shut down. It is against humanity." This was not just talk. They came with so-called scientific magazines and started to complain about this program in a mining area where two crazies were damaging youngsters.

They didn't check with us. They had no indications whether they were right or wrong, because *we* had no indications, either, because we never experienced this before. Yet we believe it cannot be bad. We are not overforcing the kids. They are doing it because they *can* do it and because they love it. Nothing wrong can happen. You cannot do any harm to them. We were just giving the children something that they like and which is going to benefit them.

When we first arrive in Vulcan we are watching the little miner kids doing their work at their benches, and most are very skinny and timid. But in two years they are straight and steady and they've got personality. They were smiling and they were happy. "It is worth it, our effort," I decide. But Martha got a little bit worried about it. We were at the point where we wanted to have a baby, and we had to support ourselves.

"These people come here and they are going to screw up everything," she tells me. "Who knows what is going to happen? Maybe we lose our job. Let's slow down."

"No," I said. "I can't do it. I don't want to do it. We got to make it. Look, people are happy."

But we went to the school and talked to the principal, whose name was John Illies. He was a semi–Communist Party guy; that's why he was principal. He was worried, and didn't want anything to happen. "Well, shut down a little," he decided. "We'll explain to the parents. Let's call them in this afternoon. Don't worry."

Immediately after the workout we had a meeting. The parents had no idea why they had to come, and usually they do not respond when the school asks. But because it was about gymnastics, everybody comes. Husbands come directly from the mine with their wives.

"We appreciate what these people have done," Illies tells them. "But you have to realize that we have a situation here that may later be harmful."

You know the miners. Don't step on their toes; they're aggressive. One of the old ones stands up, very angry.

"Listen you," he tells the principal. "I am sixty years old and never in my life have I seen anything like this, what they're doing. God bless them." Then he looks at his pickax. "I cut your head off in a second. Don't touch them."

Suddenly, everybody started to jump up, and it was like a revolt. "It's our kids," they shouted. "Our kids."

Well, it was our first big victory. A fight of the concept. There is great satisfaction knowing that behind you is lined up the whole community.

So in the third year we start to dominate with authority the whole nation, winning competition after competition. We were so powerful, we could line up six good teams at the same time. There is no way to beat us. The next year the Romanian gymnastics federation introduces a new rule, creating a junior and senior division.

Of course, there is nobody in the junior division but ourselves.

For three years in a row we are competing alone, lining up four or five of our own teams just to make it some kind of an event. But the good part is that elsewhere in Romania other people started to listen, to show interest and to start programs for the young ones. And finally, in the fifth year, they start a program for them that involves the whole country. This is how happens the Romanian revolution in gymnastics.

Suddenly we get a call from the Education Ministerium, which is separate from the Sport Ministerium. Our principal comes to me during a workout and tells me there is important phone call. My God, I think, they are going to shut us down. Instead, it is the opposite.

"Listen," the lady tells me, "you guys are doing an outstanding job and I strongly believe it works."

Well, we talk a little bit. She was Maria Login, the chief of the sports department of the Education Ministerium, and she says she wants to come up and see our program. After a few months she does, and she observes this little-bitty gymnasium with the homemade apparatus, full with kids.

"We've been giving this some thought," she says, "and we have some funds. How about we are giving you an opportunity to join a national institute of gymnastics that we are putting together?"

This is better than a dream, I tell myself, but I really don't know if I am ready.

"I have no experience as an administrator," I tell her, "and I don't know if I can help."

"Don't worry about that," she assures me. "We can hire a few other people. We will have an administrator, a manager, all these services. Because we want to set up a special school with an educational and physical program together. You can start next month."

This is unbelievable, I think. Fantastic. This is in August of 1968, and we begin looking around the country for a suitable place. There were several big towns that were very interested to have us, but they couldn't support financially the program we wanted. We needed not only a gymnasium but also a school building, dormitories, teachers, and coaches. Those were our requirements. Finally, my attention

31

was captured by a very remote chemical-industrial town up by the Russian border on the other side of the country.

The place was called Onesti, and although it had only been settled for ten or twelve years, it already had about forty-five-thousand people, and was growing unbelievably fast. The population was a mixture of intellectuals, middle-class people, agriculture workers, so there wasn't a traditional educational atmosphere like Transylvanian towns, which had a very strict conservative mentality. Onesti was both aggressive and progressive, and the people there were very enthusiastic. They wanted to have something outstanding there, and they would make a full effort.

Their mayor was a young, ambitious person named Valeriu Ghinet, who wanted to climb in the political hierarchy, and he really wanted to help, too. So in a very short time they gave us one building for the school, another for dormitories, and put up the money for a beautiful new gymnasium.

As soon as everything was ready I started to go around looking for kids. Of course, we offered a lot of advantages for a six- or seven-year-old in Romania—education, housing, meals, equipment, coaching all for free. If we were offering that much, we had the right to choose the best ones, and I was very picky.

Some of the kids came with me from my little mining town of Vulcan. Others came from gymnastics centers elsewhere in the country. They weren't well-known international gymnasts, but they were experienced, so we could get involved right away in competitions.

But our main concern was to develop our first generation of young gymnasts, the six- and seven-year-olds who would be our nucleus. So I went with Martha through all the kindergartens in that area, looking for children who could be gymnasts. Not just in Onesti, where there were six or seven kindergartens, but in the suburban villages, too. We must have screened twenty-five-thousand kids, always making larger and larger the circle. For two or three hours each morning and every Saturday and Sunday I would take my bicycle and observe children from kindergarten and first grade at play. Of course, my eye was mostly catching those who were playing at gymnastics and not something else.

One day, watching a group of kids, I noticed two blonde-headed girls who were throwing cartwheels better than anyone else. They were just playing and not making any effort to show off. But when recess was over I lost track of them. I went through each class, trying to find them, but I could not. So I went through again, asking questions this time.

"Who likes gymnastics?"

"I like, I like," some of them would say.

"Well, let me see your faces," I'd tell them, trying to figure which ones were the ones I'd seen. I'd set them aside and see which of them could do cartwheels and handstands. No use.

"I know there were two little ones," I told the principal. "Let me go through one more time."

"You have already been through ten times," she argued. "You have already asked everyone who likes gymnastics."

"Once more," I pleaded.

So I went through again, and this time I try a new method.

"Let me see your eyes," I told the kids, just to get them to look at me. Of course, many of them are not paying attention. But finally I see one little girl looking up at me out of the corner of her eyes.

"Ahhh, come here buddy," I tell her. "Let me see you do a cartwheel."

Sheeeoom, she does a perfect one. And that was how I found Nadia Comaneci. "Little buddy," I ask, "where the other one is? Your friend."

"Oh," Nadia says, "she's in another class."

"Okay. Get me her."

Well, her friend, whose name was Viorica Dumitru, was even better. Later she became one of Romania's greatest ballerinas. So we picked them up and put them in our program, and we worked all fall. It was a beautiful start, with everything clean, everything new, everything fresh, and those little bugs already doing good gymnastics. Those were exciting times for us. Everything was new for me—organization, administration, placing the funds in the right direction. And with the little ones we make great progress.

The best years for gymnastics are between seven and eleven. Those are beautiful years, so efficient and so good, because you are working with children who are one-hundred percent dedicated, one-hundred percent go-for-it. There are no limitations, not many bad thoughts, no crashes. Everything is positive, and you can see on their faces the pleasure of performing. Later, when they start to get into puberty, they begin to think and to become more conservative. "Wait," the teenage girl tells herself. "I am cute. What for I am falling on my face and bending my nose?"

But until that point they are going freely. The young ones have no fear of performing difficult skills. They never experience accidents or injuries, so they ignore the danger. And they are so light that they fall in many different ways but never get hurt.

Some people said that we were killing those kids, overforcing them in workouts. But we never did that. We just let them go. Our philosophy was that nothing can happen wrong while the kid is showing positiveness.

We discovered that you cannot overwork young children. When I was a kid, I was all the time running around. "You are going to destroy yourself," my mother warned me.

"Let the child go," my father told her. "There is an automatic system, like electronics. When the child is tired, he sits down. There is no way to move him. But in a few seconds he is getting up and continuing."

This, I find out, is absolutely true. You can see the little two-year-olds going boom-boom-boom. They relax for a moment, then go boom-boom-boom again. But if you force them, forget it. You can pull the skin off them and they are still not doing it. You can do it with adults. You can stand behind them with a shotgun and force them to work their butts off. Not the child.

The only thing that consistently works with kids is to stand behind them, motivate them, make them excited. You show the challenge, make them feel confident, and that makes them to be going further and further all the time. That was our approach from the beginning. "Yes," we told our girls. "You're gonna make it. We're gonna make it. Yes. Make it. Now or never."

It is all these minor encouragements that build them up to pass personal limits, to get them to believe that they are capable of a super effort. After a while you have a gymnasium full of roosters, tough and confident and nasty, ready to fight you.

Well, after a couple of years, we are ready to go out with our little team for competitions. We already had four or five little stars, and one was Nadia, but she wasn't the best of them. Her school friend, Dumitru, was brilliant, making excellent progress. And there was another little girl named Maria Cojanu who was also a strong competitor.

The first time we went out for a competition, Nadia finished around twelfth or thirteenth, so her start was not the most incredible one. It was pretty timid, in fact. So I was not at all sure she'd ever be the best of them. Nadia held back everything. She never showed her emotions. But she was an extremely hard worker and a bright kid. She would always follow advice, would try hard to make it, and had an amazing potential for work.

In the same time somebody else could do a skill or a movement three times, Nadia could do it six times. Her volume-per-workout was always double anybody else's. So gradually, progress came for her. By the end of her third year with us Nadia began to be the most consistent gymnast we had. And when we went to Sofia in 1972 for the Friendship Cup, our first major international, she made a huge sensation.

The Friendship Cup includes all those countries who are powerful in gymnastics—the Soviet Union, East Germany, Czechoslovakia, Hungary, Bulgaria, Poland. Nobody expected anything from us, since Romania had never been a strong competitor in the sport.

But Nadia is like flying squirrel. She wins the all-around, the bars, the vault, the floor exercise, and makes a great impression. And we beat the Russians for the first time. Everybody was shocked. It was considered an accident. Nobody could explain how we came away with a huge trophy. But our little team just bulldozered them down.

Well, in 1973 we beat them again, like horses. And in 1974 after we beat them again, there was no more question. The East Germans immediately sent technical crews down to search how this thing happens. The Russians, you know how they are. Their ego didn't allow them to come down. But they pulled information from every-where.

What they learn is that it is not only Nadia. We also have Teodora Ungureanu, who may be even better. We have Anca Grigoras, Georgeta Gabor, Mariana Constantin, several others. By now the Russians are in a panic. They just couldn't believe that our victory in 1972 marked a turnover in their hundred-year-hegemony, that it was the beginning of the end. They had considered it an aberration, that their team had only had a bad day. They couldn't understand that from then on they had to face a very dangerous adversary.

You have to realize that the Russians had dominated women's gymnastics since they first showed up at the 1952 Olympics. They had a gymnastics-making engine, like a huge factory, thousands of clubs with hundreds of thousands of athletes, all following the same plans and using the same methodology. It wasn't easy to overthrow that engine, but it happened because we were willing to go our own way, to go against the world trend which had everybody following the Russians.

We did it the most natural way, by working hard and preparing our athletes both physically and mentally, and opening our minds to new technical possibilities. I had never wanted to follow anybody. I never could, because I hadn't had a strong gymnastics background. So I had no formula, no idol, no traditional scheme. What I followed was based on a simple reality: the kids are the best teachers.

You can learn more from them than from any kind of books, and I recognized that at the beginning. Anybody who has a clear mind and is not an egomaniac can learn. If you have open eyes you can see in a short time that the kids are guiding you to the most efficient way. I knew certain technical information from my studies at the physical education institute in Bucharest, where gymnastics was my specialty. Studying biomechanics helped. But no one book can teach you better than the kids.

I did develop a few very efficient techniques and the methodology to teach them. But eventually it just became a matter of continual development of the basic skills. We were always going further, further, further. Polishing moves. Perfecting one skill makes possible a new one. We would introduce a turn, a twist, an additional movement, and suddenly you had a new skill. All the time, of course, our kids are growing bigger and incorporating these new skills naturally. And I knew, just as two and two makes four, that if our gymnasts are stronger and more explosive, that they'll perform better. So we put heavy emphasis on conditioning, because that helps build consistency.

And we work intensively on the mental aspect, too. You see so many kids who are great athletes but they are timid, like scared rabbits. And when the fight comes, is coming a little rooster and killing them. So we wanted fighters. Never give up, we tell our girls. In no situation give up. This is not something we introduce for half an hour. It is built up through a long period of time. You see the desire in the eyes, the willingness to respond to you, to be nasty.

We work on all these things, and in six years we developed a new kind of gymnast—very athletic, aggressive, and powerful, and doing difficult skills. There was nothing mysterious or overscientific about it. It was simply a new approach. We never copied anybody else. If you copy, you will never be first. You will only be a poor imitation of the best.

In the meantime the Russians were sticking with their older athletes who had done so well for them in world championships and Olympic Games.

They were still using Lyudmila Turishcheva, Elvira Saadi, Olga Korbut, and others who were all excellent gymnasts but relatively old ladies. They weren't over the hill, but they were very close to their limit. The Russians thought that by improving them or just pushing them harder, they could reestablish their dominance. So they introduced killing workouts, seven or eight hours a day, but it didn't work.

The big problem was that their girls were already fully formed. These big old ladies could only make so-called belly-beat action-based skills on the uneven bars, but our little bugs are making already release movements *between* the bars. They can do all these amazing new moves up there—release movements, front and back somersaults, twisting movements.

They'd never even been tried before. The concept was that nobody could do it, but Nadia came with her flips and her sensational dismounts, and she opened a new technical era. She and the rest of our girls were simply younger, had more potential, and were in full progress.

Well, the Russians and East Germans woke up and desperately started to reach down and work with the younger generation, but they couldn't make up the difference quickly enough. We had an advantage of four or five years, and that was too much of a handicap for them.

They can sense the beginning of the end at the European championships of 1975, when Nadia, at thirteen years old, beats Turishcheva, who had been the Olympic all-around champion in 1972. The only weapon they can use against us is the rule book, which is exactly what they do. In 1976, the year of the Olympic Games, the Russians pushed through a new rule that you had to be fourteen to compete internationally.

The reason, of course, is that they had run out of powerful young people. They had their excellent older generation, but most of them were twenty-one or older. By introducing the minimum age of fourteen, the Russians intended to knock out Nadia's generation. But what the Russians couldn't do, our own Romanian federation had done in 1974, making the minimum age of fourteen and knocking us out of all the international competitions that year.

The jealousies, you see, had already begun. The big clubs in Bucharest—especially Dynamo, which represented the security forces—were very upset because they had lost their supremacy to us, and were also giving up places on the national team. So they made a huge opposition and put pressure on the federation guys, who were government people and didn't want to take the chance of not having good relations with Dynamo. And they told us we were too young to compete internationally. Which meant that, competitively, 1974 was a completely dead year for us. But in another way it was an excellent year because we could prepare without any kind of pressure, stress, or rush.

We had already gone to Paris after the 1974 world championships for an exhibition, and Nadia and Ungureanu made a great impres-

38

sion, receiving standing ovations. Well, the public quickly forgot about Turishcheva and the Russians. The reaction was like a fire going around the world. Who are these kids? And that was how the craziness started.

There was a great controversy within the established gymnastics community. The chairman of the technical committee of the international federation was an old Hungarian woman, and her mind was filled with visions of nice butterflies and ballet dancers. When the lady saw our kids doing their flips, she was very disturbed. "Is attempt at suicide," she said. "Whoever is pushing them to do this is a criminal." This is the same woman who in 1972, when Korbut for the first time did a back somersault on the beam, said that it was craziness, a circus, a degenerating of gymnastics, and had to be prohibited.

But progress never can stop. The wheel is going, and nobody can halt the will of the times. This new trend which was rolling, rolling, rolling, just rolled over her and she ended up her time looking like a fool.

But she was not the only one. There was pretty heavy and violent opposition from within our sport. Nobody wanted to accept this new trend. Nobody wanted to see very young people taking over from the older ones. Nobody wanted to disturb the old-fashioned classical style based on static movements and choreography combined with easy tumbling and acrobatic skills. Nobody wanted to make their life more complicated.

Whenever you come out with something new and successful, many people say, no, you are going to be a failure. These are persons who are lazy and don't want to work hard, and all my life they have been making these predictions. They are the same people who last year were saying that Mary Lou is like a fat fireplug sitting on a New York street corner. In 1975 they were saying that our kids were going to look like crippled dogs. Even when our success was well established, articles were coming out about the crazy Communist torture, the miraculous and mystical way the Russians and Romanians prepared their gymnasts.

This was understandable, because for the Western countries there was hardly any way to get into our countries to study what was going on. It wasn't allowed. So those people, especially the Americans and English, began to talk about tormenting and starving, about drugs and forced environments and concentration camps. Nobody can realize that it is merely a sound system based on hard work, government support, and progressive techniques.

In any case, by 1975 everybody, including the Russians, realize there is no way to stop us. We went to Montreal for the pre-Olympic competition, and Nadia and Ungureanu sweep away everybody. At the European championships that year Turishcheva went down like a bullet before Comaneci, and it was virtually the end of her career.

What people do not realize is that Ungureanu is basically the equal of Nadia, but she has had very bad luck at important times. In 1972 when we beat the Russians in the Friendship Cup at Sofia, Teodora did not make our team and it is Nadia who makes the great sensation. In 1973 Ungureanu won almost everything she entered but just before the Friendship Cup she has her tonsils removed. In 1975 she missed the European championships with the flu. If she had been healthy, maybe Nadia does not go on to become such a big Olympic star.

So chance was always following Nadia. But as the proverb says, most of the time you are making your own chance, and Nadia was an unbelievable hard worker. She was strong-willed and one-hundred percent dedicated. If Nadia was sick she wouldn't even pay attention to it. She would have a high fever all week and we'd never find out. Her mother would have to tell us, because we could never see it in her performance in the gym.

People said she had no emotions, and it is true that Nadia's basic personality wasn't too open. She was a kid raised in pretty hard conditions in a family without much everyday love or fun. But she was a hard-working, determined, excellent athlete. Nadia's world was smaller than most people's; she grew up in the gym. Her friends were the girls she knew from there and from the dormitories.

I didn't try to change her personality, because at that time I think it could have been a mistake and ended up a big mess. My mentality and hers was very much the same: Go and make it. Go and do it. Don't joke around. Forget everything else. Take one-hundred percent seriously your job; that is what you have been working for.

So when we came to Montreal for the 1976 Olympic Games Nadia felt excellently confident. The women's technical committee of the international gymnastics federation had kicked out all the male coaches from the floor during the women's competition, but it did not matter. Nadia felt just as she had at home, because we had developed that over long years of preparation and competition.

Now I didn't know what to expect at Montreal because the Olympics are so different from any other competition. No world championship or World Cup is anything like it. The atmosphere captures you and from the moment you step into the village, you are flying, you are having goose bumps. The public and the media are pushing you up into seventh heaven. But Nadia is able to ignore all this and put together a fantastic performance.

On the first day, in the compulsory exercises, she scores a perfect 10 on the bars, the first in Olympic history. The next night, in the optionals, Nadia gets two more 10s, in bars and beam, and brings us to the team silver medal behind the Russians, who have three gold medalists from 1972—Turishcheva, Korbut, and Saadi—on their team.

In the all-around final, where no Romanian girl has ever won as much as a medal, Nadia makes two more 10s and captures the gold, beating Nelli Kim and Turishcheva and Korbut and all the rest.

Then, in the apparatus finals, she completes her triumph. Nadia gets yet another 10 on the bars, and beats Ungureanu for the gold medal there. She earns a 10 on the beam, and beats Korbut, who was defending champion. Then she wins a bronze in the floor exercise, and finishes fourth in the vault.

So Nadia finishes the week with three gold medals, a silver, and a bronze. But more impressively, she piles up seven perfect scores where nobody before her manages even one. Of course, in a subjective sport there has never been perfection, and it is hard to tell what is absolute perfection. But at the time, what Nadia did was considered perfect. They couldn't find anything wrong with it.

So the Montreal Olympics are an unbelievable success for Romania. Besides what Nadia does, Ungureanu wins the silver medal on bars, and the bronze on the beam. And in the team competition we beat the East Germans, the Hungarians, the Czechs—all of the socialist countries except for the Soviet Union.

In all of Olympic history our women have only won two bronze medals before this, and none since 1960. What we achieve in 1976 we achieve after only eight years with a program we start from the bottom, and we do it using kids.

It is, as everybody says, a miracle, a new era in gymnastics. But as we find when we return home, nothing will ever be the same again.

BELA

The End of a Life

After the Olympic Games our whole country is in festivity. Huge celebrations, banquets, President Ceauşescu calling personally—all these things. They never give out the highest order of communism, The Hero of Socialist Labor, to actors or artists or athletes, but they give it to us. Great satisfactions; the whole country is crazy.

But there is also bad side—jealousies. The Romanian gymnastics federation gets frustrated because they felt they were not recognized or compensated for what they did. So they become number-one enemies of us, and that is how the tragedy started.

One of the top federation officials thought it would be easy to resolve the situation. Just pull out the team and put it in Bucharest. Then our community will not have any kind of influence or get any more recognition. *They* will get all the recognition. Unfortunately, other people feel the same way. The Education Ministerium, they are proud because they initiate the program. And the Communist government, they want to have Nadia over there, to share in her fame and show her at various meetings.

Already, she was a huge international star. Arabian sheiks, kings, presidents come almost every day asking to meet personally Nadia. So the pot is boiling in Bucharest, but we had no idea what was going on. We were just working out in Onesti, and after three months I just shut down all the visits. I kicked out everybody.

"No," I tell them, "we are not trained clowns. We cannot run a sports program in this way. The kids get tired, I get tired. We want to go in our own way."

So I decided no TV, no journalists, nobody, except for once a month. We would have an open press conference so everybody can come in and ask questions for an hour. Well, it was like I cut off my own thumb, like I kill myself. That was the end.

Overnight the government and the federation begin to talk to the parents. They tell them how important it is for them to be in the capital. How it is lifetime chance to be around the president, to have a fine living situation, to get good jobs, good houses, cars, lots of compensation.

"This crazy Karolyi," they tell the parents, "he has lost his mind. He is kicking out people who want to admire your child."

So step by step, those people who were standing so close behind us, they agree with the government. And one evening, without any kind of notice, the whole team was picked up and taken to Bucharest. They had already set up the whole thing. A brand-new center. Coaches, masseurs, doctors—everything. A big celebration in the capital, where the government guys are waiting for them with flowers. And we are at home, we have no idea.

Well, the next day is a Sunday, when we always have a morning workout. The kids were all the time playing crazy games and jokes, sneaking into the gym and hiding and I had to find them. So it is 9 o'clock and I open the building and am standing around.

"Aha, there is nobody here," I say in a loud voice. "I am going home." Nothing. No sound. Usually, they are hiding in the pit. So I jump in—"Heeeyyy"—and nobody is there. Where the hell they are? I ask myself. Martha was doing some paperwork in the other office. "Did we schedule something, some exhibition, and forget?" I ask her. "Is anything we do not remember?"

"No," she says.

So I call up the parents. "Hey," I ask the first one, "Where the girls are?"

"Ah, you know," he says, "they got to be around. Yesterday somebody was here. One of the federation guys."

"What was he doing?"

"Well, you know," he says, "he was talking to the girls."

"Talking to the girls? Not to me? Where he is?"

"I believe they left yesterday evening," he tells me.

"They were here and they left?"

Oh, my god, I say to myself. So I call the second parents, and the third, and they are not home. Finally one parent tells me. "Yeah, they left yesterday," he says. "For Bucharest."

"No, no way," I say. "This is bad joke."

So I went to the mayor, Ghinet, and told him, and he was shocked. "No," he says. "This cannot happen without my knowledge." So he calls up and gets confirmation. Yes, they were in Bucharest because they were national treasure and they've got to be there with the best conditions.

"This town didn't give them best conditions?" I ask him. "This town made them what they are. This town made them Olympic champions. Why don't they consult me?"

Well, after this the whole community that had supported us gradually lost interest. The mayor, who was a good friend, lost faith in everybody, including me.

"You knew it," he accused me. "You *had* to know it. You agreed to do it. You were in the same boat with those crooks."

"Look," I told him, "if I knew it, I would be there. But I'm here with you, trying to survive."

It was awful. Can you imagine taking away a whole Olympic team? It was like earthquake. The whole town was very quiet. No questions, nothing. It was a touchy area to talk about. But I tried to make it as best I could. I spent more hours than ever in the school, trying to keep things together and get everybody excited again. But it was impossible. I had lost the credit of the people. After a few months we realize there is no way. I was so disappointed and depressed, I decide to give up and move back to our little coal-mining area.

So I call the mayor there, my old friend. "Hey," I ask him, "do you want two physical education teachers?"

"Bela," he says, "you crazy guy. Sure I do. Come back. We build the greatest gymnasium in the world, anything you want. We put skyscrapers up for you. Come home, come home."

So I say to my wife, we must do it. Martha is very conservative, she never wants big changes. "No," she says, "we have responsibilities here."

"Well," I say, "there is responsibility today, but not necessarily tomorrow. I don't think anybody will mind. I don't think anybody is interested anymore. Nobody is walking in the door. Before, it was in and out every day. Now, nobody even steps into this place. So tomorrow, we are going."

So I talked to the mayor of Onesti. "My decision is to leave," I inform him. "It is too disappointing, the most frustrating thing ever to happen in my life. I just don't want to be here anymore."

"I can't blame you if you want to go," Ghinet says. "Just find someone to keep the school going."

So I call up the Ministerium and tell them I am leaving. I arrange the details. And in February of 1977 we go back to Vulcan, where the whole town, all those miners, comes out. A big parade is organized, a huge celebration, because it had been more than eight years.

So, I start to get ambitions again. I get my speed back and put big plans together, because besides us there are three gymnastics centers in the country, lots of competition. We build a new gymnasium, in Deva, which is the capital of the region. A quality setup, with a school, a cafeteria, everything we need. The best teachers from the town will be involved and we have one-hundred percent cooperation from the school to assure that we will have the best selection of the kids.

In a month and a half we have organized everything. Before long the dormitory is built. The gymnasium is up, a big, beautiful facility. Besides, I had brought with me all the best juniors from our school in Onesti. So we already had a good team, and we speeded up our program with great ambitions. After a year and a half we have a very competitive group.

By now it is October of 1978, and time for the Romanian championships. We hadn't signed up for them because we had only juniors, but Martha and I realized we were the dumbest people in the world if we didn't.

"But these kids don't know compulsories," Martha worried.

"I know," I said.

"But we have only a few weeks."

"So? We try. We cannot lose too much. We try. We still have five weeks to work."

Now, the federation had never given us any opportunities for international competition after the Olympics. But through the mayor of Deva and the Ministerium we put on some pressure, and finally the federation says, okay, go to Cuba for the Friendship Cup if you want to.

Well, the Russians had been celebrating ever since they heard the team had been taken away from me. "Never worry about the Romanians," they said. "They never will beat us again." And that is exactly what had happened.

The team that had been taken away never showed up for any competition because they'd never been prepared. Those kids are going down, worse and worse. Half of them were already injured. Nadia's size was growing unbelievable. She is deformed, like a fat elephant. She gained twenty kilos, more than forty pounds. Can you imagine? Literally, she couldn't move. The other kids, like Teodora Ungureanu, get into the crazy big-town life in Bucharest. Celebrations, parties, personal appearances, chasing boys every night. They get lost, totally confused.

At the same time my young ones, they get oxygen. They think they have a chance to accomplish something. So we go to the Friendship Cup and we beat again the Russians, and they are shocked. "There is no way this can happen," the Russians tell me. "You moved, you give up, you're dead."

We return to Bucharest three days before the national championships. Don't go home at all, we decide. Stick here, rent hotel rooms, work out in a nearby gymnasium, and wait.

Well, everything works unbelievable well. After the first day we are in first place, beating our former team by more than seven points in compulsories, which is a fantastic margin in gymnastics. So we knew it was over, because nobody could touch us in optionals. No way to do it.

Martha and I go back to our room and have a cup of schnapps and are talking happily. Suddenly there is knock on the door.

"Come in," I say. Nobody comes. Again, a knock. So Martha goes to the door and standing there is a big, fat girl. I swear I did not recognize her. Then she opens her mouth and it is Nadia. Such mixed feelings. After so many months to see that disaster there in the doorway. She came in, and started to cry.

"Nadia, Nadia," I ask. "What the hell happened?"

"I want to give my life up," she says.

It was true. She did have a suicide attempt, drinking a liquid detergent. She was desperate, totally confused. Somebody who just a year before was a world-famous star, sweetheart of everybody, was literally hiding because she didn't want to show her face, to have people recognize her. She was a sorrow.

"Help me," she pleaded. "I want to go back with you."

"Nadia, we have moved," I told her. "We are not anymore there. We are in another part of Transylvania."

"I want to go anywhere," she insisted. "Just let me go with you."

"There is no way to make it," I said. "The time is over. I wrote off the federation. I don't have anything to do with them. The team, all your friends, is here. We cannot fit you in the program. We have no seniors, no big girls. My little ones, like Emilia Eberle, are working like crazy, like engines. Besides, Nadia, if you make this decision, can you commit yourself to work like never before in your life? I don't know how you can do it. You feel you are capable for such hard work?"

"I don't care," she said. "I hate myself, I hate everybody. I want to die. I just want to go back and be with you."

"Nadia," I said, "I cannot make that decision. I will talk to some people and get some information."

In the morning I went out and walked around the city, and thought about the situation. What would everybody think, me having Nadia back? It would create such a big problem. I was confused.

Then at our workout the same federation guy who was responsible for taking the team away from me shows up. Big smile, very friendly.

"Hello, Bela, good to see you," he begins. "Such a long time. Let's have lunch and talk."

"I'm not interested in talking," I say. "I'm in the middle of a competition."

"Well," he says, "the president of the national sports federation wants to talk to you."

"I am not interested," I say.

"You sure?"

"I am very sure. I am positive."

I say good-bye and turn my back and walk away. Still, I am thinking about my conversation with this man, and about Nadia. The guy is shameless to come to me smiling. I could not do to anyone what he does to me.

That night we win the competition by sixteen points, we take the first six places, plus ninth. A total success. Afterwards I feel a tapping on my shoulder. It is the president of the Romanian sports federation, a general named Dragnea. He was a pretty fair guy, and I respected him.

"Congratulations, Bela," he tells me. "You do it again."

"Well," I say, "it is what we like to do."

"Why don't you take the team back?" he suggests, "and prepare them for the world championships?"

"What kind of team are you talking about?" I wondered.

"You know, the national team."

"Did you see this competition?" I ask him. "Do you think any of that team can go to the world championships and line up against the Russians?"

"Not necessarily those guys," Dragnea says. "I was thinking about your team."

"Not my guys. They are juniors. They aren't old enough."

"Ahh, I can make them fifteen," he says. "I can arrange. I just want you to take on the national team because I am sick of what is going on here."

"Never," I say.

"Well, I order you to," he says. "If you don't, it is not in the best interests of the country and the sport, and I don't know how we will regard your new school."

"You destroy my school," I tell him, "you destroy my life. You want to threaten me? Doesn't work, because I don't care. The community doesn't care. We are supporting ourselves."

On the way back to the hotel Martha and I talk. We realize they can influence negatively the center. They can hurt us. We know that. We will never get competitions, and we can never give satisfactions to the kids. Our jobs and our whole lives will be worthless. At the same time there is Nadia. What the hell to do with her?

"We've got to," Martha decides. "They can kill us."

"No," I say. "We won't."

As the kids are packing their luggage and we are getting ready to go back to Deva, a man comes up.

"Mr. Karolyi?"

"Yes?"

"Come downstairs. Someone is waiting for you."

It was the former mayor of a nearby industrial town to Vulcan who now had become one of the biggest Party personalities.

"You know I have always supported you," he tells me. "I appreciate what you did and what you are doing now in your little town. But I am advising you, friendly, firmly, and frankly, to take back the national team and work again. We have the reports, and the whole sports picture of Romania is in danger. There is no team. The world championships are coming up in five weeks and there is nothing. If we don't move up in the world rankings, we are done forever. We are laughingstock of the world. Look at this picture of Nadia."

"You don't have to show," I tell him. "I saw her yesterday."

"You take the national team," he says, "and start to prepare."

"It cannot be done," I insist. "Five weeks? I'm not a magician, I cannot do it. You don't understand. Nadia was not even in the competition here. The other five members of the team were worse than sixth place. They are doing nothing. There is no way to prepare them."

"Take anyone, then. That is my frank advice. Do it."

So I went back to my room. "You don't have to tell me what he said," Martha tells me. "I knew it."

I found Nadia and told her to take her luggage, that we were going to begin again.

Well, it was a five-week nightmare. I never did it before in my life, and I would never do it again. To teach the young ones compulsories at the international level. To make Nadia, who was like elephant, to look like human being again. To get her into simplified routines, to exercise somehow. To get her into shape at least to move. It was unbelievable. I was running miles with her every day. Massage, running, massage, sauna, running, going back and forth like crazy. She had been out of gymnastics for five months. Absolutely nothing, not even lifting her leg. But she loses thirty-five pounds, and finally she is ready.

So we go to Strasbourg, and get second place as a team, doing it with Nadia and some unknown kids like Eberle, who is thirteen years old but wins three medals. In all, we take five medals, one of them gold, so you can imagine the satisfaction.

It was not a voluntary thing, it was forced, but Nadia is in fantastic condition for the second time in her life, winning the beam. In 1979 we win everything. At the European championships Nadia beats Elena Mukhina, the new Soviet star, and we sweep away the whole Russian crew, going 1-2-4 in the all-around, killing them.

We go to the world championships in Fort Worth that year, with all these young ones lining up behind Nadia, all these little bugs nobody knew before. Eberle, Melita Ruhn, Cristina Grigoras, Rodica Dunca, Dumitrita Turner.

The first day we are doing well, but Nadia develops an infection in her left hand. In the morning it is all red and swollen. So she goes to the hospital to have the hand drained and bandaged. When she returns to the gym our team is already warming up for the optional competition, preparing without her.

With her hand the way it was, Nadia could not do vaulting,

tumbling, or go on the bars. So the Russians and East Germans are jubilating, figuring that she is effectively out. And our little ones, they are sitting with long faces, thinking that we have no chance.

"No, buddies," I tell them. "We are handicapped, but not defeated. This is lifetime chance for you. How long you are doing gymnastics? Six years? Seven? Well, this is the moment you have been working so hard for. *Now* begins your time. Let's go out and take it. Will you go for it, Emilia? Will you go for it, Dumitrita? Cristina? Rodica? Melita? Yes. Sure, we gonna do it. We *got* to do it. Now or never."

Well, our little bugs are going for it, performing fantastic routines with no mistakes. And Nadia with unbelievable courage gets up and does a beam routine on one hand, scoring a 9.95.

In the meantime the Russians are falling from the bars. They are cautious in their floor routines. And we beat them for the championship, the first time the Russians had lost at the world level since 1966. Besides that, Eberle wins the gold medal in floor exercise, Ruhn the bronze in the all-around, and Turner finishes first in vault.

The competition is a great success for us. When we go back home the whole country falls in love again, especially with Nadia. She was exciting to watch, not a child anymore, but woman. Tall, beautiful-looking, performing like goddess.

Of course, begins again the whole jealousy with the Romanian gymnastics federation and the government. They talk to her parents, who were simple people and very easy to confuse. Her mother was an ambitious one, always making demands for housing and money.

"Well," they told her, "Nadia should come to the capital to be around the president and all the activity."

So in February of 1980, five months before the Olympic Games, she moves back to Bucharest. What could I say? We were not anymore surprised. So we set about preparing the other ones. And in June Nadia shows up again. She is out of shape with wrinkles under her eyes. She looks like an old woman.

"Nadia," I say, "what are you doing?"

"Well, this is my last chance," she tells me. "You used to talk to me about a second Olympic Games. I would like to try." She was much cooler this time, less emotional.

"I just can't handle what is happening to me," she admitted. "I just want one more time to do it, and I promise I will never bother you again."

"Nadia," I advised her, "I would not do it. It is going to be awfully hard. You know where the Olympic Games are? In Moscow. If you go to Moscow and you are not in perfect shape, superprepared, there is no way in the world to win. And if you don't win the Olympic Games, it is worthless to even go. So you better don't.

"You've got everything. You're in better position than any athlete ever dreamed in this country. You have all the opportunities. Don't do this. We have a powerful team, we're going to get some medals anyway. Nobody will ask us if you are not there. If you are there, everyone will be after our butt. We have less than two months to prepare you. Nadia, don't do it. We cannot make it."

"I must," she said. "It is my last chance. You must help me."

"Okay," I say finally. "For the last time, we start again."

She is in poor condition, but we work hard, and when the Games start Nadia is in tremendous shape, the best-looking gymnast there by far.

Well, the Western countries are boycotting, and the Russians line up two thousand soldiers right on the bleachers who are booing anybody in the world except their own gymnasts, transforming the competition into a circus.

What happened there you could not imagine happening in the Olympic Games. The judges, all from Socialist countries, are against the Romanians. The Russian girls are falling from the beam and still getting high scores. Elena Davidova loses her balance, and stops three times. Each one is supposed to be a four-tenths deduction, but they still give her a 9.85.

Now Nadia is coming up on the beam, her best event, where she never gets less than 10 since 1976. She is unbelievable, but they give her a 9.85. It is obvious she is Olympic all-around champion, but they take it away and give it to Davidova. I just couldn't handle any more, so we stop the whole competition and make a big protest. For forty minutes the entire Olympic Games are halted with reporters running around, pictures, everything.

We do not win, but we go home like heroes. We did something nobody else ever did, to scream and yell in Moscow against the Russians. But I did it, and it was appreciated at that time in our country. In a competition you go with your child. You are morally obligated to do everything to help her. Be nice to one judge, be cruel to another. Play games. Fight, twist necks, stand on your head, do anything. Whatever is necessary.

But three or four days later our federation people came home and said that what I had done was an anti-Communist activity. That stopping the competition, which was a Communist Olympic Games, had disturbed the whole smooth, friendly manner of the event. So in Bucharest they tell me that the Communist Party doesn't at all appreciate what I did, that even worse, my behavior is no example for the young generation. And they firmly advise me to revise my attitude.

"Listen," I told them. "For thirteen years I am fighting for this country as a team coach. I am making this country look better in athletics than ever before. I went to Moscow and I am trying to save what you call a national treasure—Nadia. I was fighting for her, for something that is pride for this country. I try to stop an unbelievable injustice which was going on under everybody's eyes. You *know* what was going on up there. We still get seven medals, two of them gold. Well, you don't have to call my attention because I am resigning. Right now. Good-bye."

I went home, and they started to play the games. The portion of my budget that comes from the government disappears overnight. Four teachers resigned from my school. Something like that happened every day, surprise after surprise after surprise. Situations you would not believe.

"I am fighting," I tell myself. "I am not giving up. They will not kill me." So I make a written resignation, and they call me to Bucharest to discuss it.

"What the hell do you think you're doing?" one of their guys asks me in a nasty way. "Writing letters. You stay in your position until we tell you we're kicking you out. While you're eating this country's bread, you will do what *we* tell you to do."

"Well," I decide, "there is no way to argue. Nothing to do." Back home Martha and I talk, and decide to give up the school and make a living somehow. Then in February of 1981 the federation calls.

"We are setting up a tour of America," they tell me. "And you're going over there."

"I'm not going," I say. "There is no reason. You just had the European championships, and a month and a half later you're going touring? You're crazy."

"We have to make some money," they tell me, "and the Americans are giving one hundred and eighty thousand dollars. You will go over there and make it."

So they set up an exhibition for fifteen stops, night after night. A killing experience. Then we arrive at the Bucharest airport and there are more people traveling with us than the whole team. Six additional persons—a federation guy, two security people, even judges. Judges for an exhibition tour that has no judging.

For fourteen years I have had free hand as leader, coach, everything. Now the federation guy says he is leader, that everybody will follow his orders. It is a public discreditation of me. The kids were looking around, not knowing how to take it. They are laughing. Is this joke? Has something gotten crazy?

"Hey, you over there," the guy says to one of the girls. "You don't smile while I am talking."

So that was how it started. As soon as we arrive in America, the federation official is presenting himself as the personal coach of Nadia. Taking her to give interviews, making speeches night after night about how the Communist philosophy gave the gymnasts the strength to go out and win. As the tour goes on, it became very obvious to me that there was no longer a reason for me to do something which was not workable. I had no more pleasure in working hard to produce athletes. I could not do my best if we have this interference.

Well, we come to New York for the final exhibition, and after it is done I am sitting in our room with Martha and Geza Pozsar, who had been our choreographer for seven years.

Always after big events we would get together to have a glass of wine and talk over what had happened. This time the girls had done well on a bone-breaking schedule, but we were still so depressed, so down about all the crazy things that had happened. After talking for a while we come to a common idea—this is not something we wanted to do anymore. The reason had disappeared. To serve this federation guy, this trash person, did not work.

"Well," I say, "what are we going to do?"

Then Martha, the conservative one, speaks up. "We don't go back," she says. "That is the only thing we can do, to show we don't agree with this situation."

"Wait a minute," I say. "What are you talking about? For four years we work like horses to build up a good situation. Not to go back? Do you know what you're talking about? Not to go back? We're through. We lost everything."

So we talk about this all night long, putting all the arguments in the balance. Andrea, our seven-year-old daughter, is back in Romania, staying with my aunt. Geza has a wife and a two-year-old daughter there. If we don't go back, perhaps we never see them again.

Besides that, we don't have anything with us, not even two pennies to put over each other. I don't even have enough for taxicab. Back home we are pretty wealthy people. If we stay in America, our house, our car, our belongings, everything we have builded up is lost.

"You're crazy," I tell Martha.

"Okay," she shrugs. "We are going back to what we do."

"You're right," I decide. "What I am doing I don't want to do anymore. I have resigned already two times in my life. Another one would be a disaster. You cannot go against the government. You cut your own throat."

Still, the only reason we have for staying in America is a moral reason. It was very thin. We are looking to start again. But where? How? On what basis? Who's going to help? Who'll stand behind us? Does anybody want us? Or not want us? All these were open questions. None of us could even come up with a positive encouragement.

But by talking and talking, step by step, we finally arrive all three at one point. We give everything up and don't turn back. By now it is 5 o'clock in the morning and we are so tired and consumed from the discussions that we just fall asleep in the chairs in our hotel room.

I woke up half an hour later, and it was like bad dream. Where was I? I woke Martha and Geza.

"People," I tell them, "we are talking about craziness. It is 5:30 now. At 6 o'clock people will start to be moving around. We've got to make a decision."

Martha was exhausted. When we had first begun talking she had been very positive, very strong. Now she was so tired she said she could not come up with any logical reasons, and told us to make the decision.

I look at Geza. "Okay, what are we going to do?"

"I can't go back," he says. "I won't go back. If you stay, I'm going to stay with you."

"Well," I conclude, "the decision is made. We are not going back."

6

BELA

Our Own Way

The day we decide to stay in America, our plane is supposed to leave New York at noon. Martha and Geza and I have been up all night talking, thinking, making our minds up. So at 7 o'clock I go to the room where Nadia and Emilia Eberle were staying to tell them.

"Listen, kids," I say. "Here are some small things to give to Andrea. Tell her we are here, and that we will do everything to be with her in time."

"What?" says Nadia. "You are not coming back?"

"No," I tell her.

Well, the kids started to cry. It was very emotional time.

"If you are friend of mine," I tell Nadia. "If you appreciate every-thing I did for you, you shut up and don't say a word. Go, now please, and call the other girls down to the reception area."

So Nadia goes room to room, and the girls come down around 8:30. They have no idea what we are planning. They didn't realize this is the last time we are going to meet each other.

"Hey, kids, the tour is over," I begin. "You did very well. You showed everything I taught to you. Don't forget you have important events coming up. Go back, work hard, and fight to get personal recognition. It doesn't matter who's going to lead you. Listen and be good people."

Everybody was getting ready to pick up some last shopping items, so it was good-bye, good-bye, good-bye, and see you at 12 o'clock. Then Martha, Geza, and I grab our luggage and walk out of the hotel.

The security man, he has no idea. So we went to a small cafeteria somewhere and tried to talk, but we could not. We had some coffee, and were just spending the time. I don't know what we were thinking about, what we were waiting for. Finally I look at my watch. 12:30. The plane is gone. Our whole previous life is gone.

"Let's go," I say. I was exhausted now, and emotionally empty. I was thinking of the kids, of Nadia and the others. We had been through so many good times, bad times, world championships, Olympic Games. Making such great things together. Suddenly everything is over. So for a couple of hours I am walking in Manhattan like drunk. My head was going "whoooohh," I was dizzy, I had a bitter taste in my mouth.

Around 4 o'clock we go over to see Martha's aunt, who lives in an apartment a few blocks away. She had come to America in 1938 and married a lawyer and had a beautiful life. Now she was in her seventies and living alone.

Anytime we were in New York we would give her a buzz, and she was always excited to see us. This time we step inside, and the old lady is watching television.

"Ohh, disaster," she is saying. "Catastrophe. Something horrible is going on."

"What?" I ask. "Is the Romanian Embassy after us?"

"No," she says. "The president is killed."

"What do you mean?"

"The president is killed," she says. "Reagan is shot by some crazy guy. Look at the TV."

I watch the film, with Reagan being hit and people on the sidewalk and confusion all around, and I feel sick. "God, no," I say. "This can't happen. We are in the wrong place. Is a jungle in this country."

Well, Martha's aunt was very happy to see us, but her excitement did not fit the reality. She was not realizing what craziness were going on.

It is even worse the next morning, when Martha and Geza and I go to the Immigration Office. If you ever want to experience something what communism is like, how it is to deal with Socialist employees, you don't have to go to Russia or Romania. Go to Immigration. The people were rude, ignorant, lazy. Some guy eating a frankfurter says, "Get in that line over there," treating us like dog. Hundreds of different people from countries around the world are in that room, standing in line for three and four hours just to get to the window. Suddenly a little-bitty Vietnamese guy is grabbing my sleeve. "Comrade," he is saying to me, "comrade." He wanted me to fill out his form. I look at Geza, and it is such a tragicomedy we begin to laugh. "What you want, comrade?" I ask the guy in Romanian. "I don't speak English. I am just like you. I can't even fill my own form out."

It is nightmare, that day. Everybody is filling out papers, and they keep giving us back the forms, saying they are not filled out correctly. We spent eight or nine hours there, trying to get help and nobody would help. They were so hostile, and my English, I don't know one word.

We go back to the apartment and decide we have made a great mistake. "There is no way to survive here," I tell myself. "Nobody wants us here." We were hungry and dizzy and depressed. All night long we were talking, trying to figure out what we could do. Andrea is back in Deva, and we have no idea what is happening to her. We have no job, no money.

But we do have a dog. The day before we decide to stay in America, Paul Ziert, the coach of the American gymnast, Bart Conner, gave me an expensive hunting dog as a gift, which I plan to take back to Romania. So our daughter is on the other side of the world and here I am dragging the dog behind me in a portable kennel, all around Manhattan.

Well, the next day we had to go back to Immigration, and fill out the application for political asylum. At our hearing the guy asks us what kind of crime we did in our life. What are we running from? Were we arrested? Prosecuted?

"We didn't leave the country because there was somebody after us," we explain, "but because we love our profession. And that is why we are here." The guy was shaking his head.

It is so uncomfortable for us. They think we are criminals. What to do? We had no idea. In a couple of days the vice-president of the U.S. Gymnastics Federation, Les Sasvary, calls us. He had come to America from Hungary and had heard about our defection. He wanted to offer an encouraging word.

He told us it wasn't a good idea to stay in New York for many reasons. Better to go to California, where there are some gymnastics clubs and more opportunities. He put us in touch with some organizations which help immigrants, and they put together enough money to get us to Los Angeles.

Our good friend knows another person who runs the Beverly Wilshire Hotel in Beverly Hills, and he kindly says he will let us stay there ten days for free. Such an irony. We are staying at probably the most expensive hotel in the city, and we had not one penny. After a while I am so hungry that my eyes are coming out of my head like a snail's. Les Sasvary has invited us over to eat a few times, and gave us some spending money. But soon we are running out.

For those first ten days I stayed in front of the TV trying to learn English by watching people's mouths, how they were forming the words. The best program was "Sesame Street" because they were speaking slowly and there were letters on the screen and we could pick up the pronunciations somehow. English is a crazy language. One way you write, another way you speak. So it is very difficult for us to communicate.

Finally we have no money left, and begins the nightmare. "Okay," I say, "I have to take any job I can get." So I began going down to the docks where the ships came in, walking around and asking about work, helping load and unload the cargoes. But because I couldn't speak English, I couldn't negotiate, so I always got the most miserable price. Every evening I would take a bus to suburbs like Long Beach and Huntington Beach and walk from restaurant to nightclub to restaurant, looking for some work, anything, just to get a few bucks to live from one day to another.

Finally I go to one place and see this huge Russian guy. I know from his face he is of some Slav origin. "Govorityeh porusski?" I ask him.

61

He stares at me. "Where are you from?"

"Romania."

"Ah, Romania," he says. "All the criminals are coming from Romania. What you want?"

"I want job," I say.

"What do you know how to do?"

"Cleaning," I say. "Anything."

"Come back at 12 o'clock," he tells me.

"Tomorrow?"

"No, tonight."

So for the next few hours I was hanging around in that area, walking back and forth. When they close, at 12, I come back.

"Okay," the Russian guys say, "you clean over there." There were two other guys working alongside me, a Chinese and an African. I could not communicate with them; they could not talk to me.

Well, at 5 o'clock the guy comes back to check our work, and he sees some dust. "You call this clean?" he asks me. "You son of a bitch." He was repeating this phrase every other statement.

So one of the first words I learn in English is son of a bitch. It is strange to me, so I look it up in an old Romanian-English dictionary someone gave me, but I cannot find that word.

"Son, son, son," I am looking, running my finger down the page. Ah, son of somebody. Somebody's boy. Okay, good. Then I look for bitch. "Bitch, bitch, bitch, hmmm." Female dog, it says. Okay, is puppy dog, I decide. Then this guy is pretty nice with me. He is calling me little puppy dog. It is not until much later, when I start coaching in summer camps and calling the kids sons of bitches, that I find out is not a good word at all.

I must have read that old dictionary two thousand times, just to learn words. Because I realize very quickly that if you cannot speak English in America, you are nobody.

When I come here I can speak six languages. I know Hungarian, Russian, Romanian, and German very well, French okay, and Italian a little. But that means nothing in America. If you cannot explain yourself in English, you begin at the bottom.

It is horrible for the immigrant. You are an educated professional in your own country, but you come here and suddenly you are questioning who you are. A chained animal? You lose your confidence, your identity. Maybe you were a worthless person all your life, you wonder. That is why nobody will give you an opportunity now. There were just times when you couldn't think anymore.

I had been calling gymnastics clubs to see about jobs, but there was nothing. In the newspapers Don Peters, the national team coach, had been saying that the Karolyis would find it difficult to make it here. It is a different system, he said, with no government standing behind you, no subsidies. The Karolyis will never make it. I will say it wasn't a real encouragement.

Well, none of the larger clubs seemed interested when we contacted them. The reason was clear later. They didn't want us as competitors in their fields. Gradually we had to get used to and accept the professional jealousy. Maybe we were frightening to them. We had produced world and Olympic champions. Maybe some of the clubs that had not been doing a good job would feel inferior if we came there and showed a more effective way.

Meanwhile, we were approaching desperation. Not knowing English we couldn't get better jobs. So I have to take any job to support ourselves. I would work all day, then work late at night at restaurants and come back and fall into bed.

We were making such a tight expenditure that we ate very little, maybe a pretzel for a whole day. We wanted to have a little set aside to go someplace in case an opportunity came up. So we were living in cheap motel rooms, the most miserable places in the world. It took most of our spending money, but it was important. I was walking or working all day and night. And knowing what was going on in the streets, I was worried.

"Even if I am dying," I told myself, "I will at least have the poorest hotel room so we can have Martha in a relatively safe place."

Of course, we still had the dog. Wherever we went, he came with us. I fed him leftovers from the restaurants where I worked. Most of the time I didn't eat, but the dog ate. We couldn't even sell him. Who would buy a dog from somebody who cannot speak English? They would think we probably stole it.

Not being able to talk to Andrea added to our personal trauma. We didn't have the money to telephone her, and it takes many weeks to send a letter to Romania and get a reply. So we didn't know what had happened to her. Had the Romanians cut the lines or taken her away? Were they torturing her? We didn't know. Nothing did happen to Andrea, but we didn't know that.

As soon as we did not go back, the government went into our house immediately and confiscated everything. That is a common procedure when somebody defects. They let Andrea keep her personal belongings, but what belongs to a seven-year-old child? A few clothes, some dolls, a bike?

Finally, after putting money away for a few days, I have the ten or fifteen bucks it takes to call Romania. We had no telephone, of course, so I had to call from the street, changing all the money to quarters and feeding them in.

The phone rings and a strange voice responds. I believe it is a wrong number and I call the operator. "Put in another ten dollars," she says, "and dial again."

"No!" I shout. "There is no way I can dial again. That was all my money. I *know* that is the number. There has to be something wrong. Please help me."

"I'm sorry," she says.

"Please, wait a second. Let me explain to you."

And in my bad English, I try. I say that the dumb machine swallowed my money, and is my last chance to get through.

"Okay," she says, "let me dial one more time."

In a moment I hear the phone ringing in Deva, and a little voice saying, "Who is there?"

My wife and I started to cry. Martha couldn't speak, she was shaking so much. What to say? What to say to Andrea?

"When are you coming home?" she asks me.

"We can't come home. But you are going to come here."

"When am I going to come? Tomorrow?"

I groan to myself. How to explain?

"No, Andrea, not tomorrow. You have to understand. We are trying to work things out, and we will send you a ticket to ride in a big airplane. You will have new friends here and it will be nice."

"Daddy," she said in a tiny voice. "Are you sure I can go?"

What could I say? The international rules for human rights, written in Geneva, say that if both parents defect, the country has to release immediately the child. But how to make it happen? It was not so much that the Romanian government would not let Andrea come here, but that they wanted to make us go back. That was the biggest pressure. The whole game was set up to convince us, to force us to change our minds.

You see, once we left, the Romanian newspapers never even mentioned our name. It was like we never existed. That was a big mistake, because we were so popular over there that everybody was asking, Where they are? How they are? What happened with them?

It was obvious we'd been fighting with the federation, so it wasn't a hidden situation, a secret. Everybody knew. When the kids came home and talked with their parents, the whole story spread like fire.

We had called the Romanian Embassy in Washington to see about getting Andrea out. The ambassador had gotten on the phone a few times and was being super-nice. They had assured us how sympathetic they are with us, how positive they would be. "But there is no way to resolve anything over the phone," we were told. "If you want anything done regarding your daughter, you've got to come to Washington and set up a meeting at the Romanian Embassy."

It was an ultimatum, no doubt. We had to do something, and with the help of Les Sasvary we flew to Washington for the meeting, not knowing what they wanted from us.

Since we didn't know anybody, we just showed up at the State Department, because we had heard that sometimes they provide an FBI agent if you're a defector and have to go to your embassy. The embassy, of course, is Romanian territory, and they can do with you anything they want. They can pick you up and send you back, and nobody can interfere. If you disappear after being with an FBI agent, though, at least somebody knows.

So we were wandering around among all the offices. Suddenly a person stopped in the corridor next to us.

"You're Romanians?" he said. "Hey, what you doing here?"

We explained that we had defected three weeks earlier and were trying to find somebody to help.

"Sure," he says. "You were those guys with Nadia. Good. I'll try to help you."

This person, whose name was Steve Gereben, was one of the members of a Hungarian freedom fighters' organization, and he had a lot of connections in Washington. "Let me take you guys somewhere to somebody who can help you," he says, and he brings us up to Capitol Hill to see a congressman from Texas named Bill Archer.

"Come in," says this smiling short person, and in our few words of English we try to explain what we are doing.

"You don't have to explain anything," Bill tells us. "I know who you are. You guys are the gymnastics coaches. My daughter and son were going crazy for Nadia. I know you better than you think. So, what's the problem?"

We tell him about our daughter and Geza's wife and child.

"Well, I don't believe it will be a big problem," he says. "I am a member of the committee of the most-favored-nations for some of the eastern European countries, and I am dealing very frequently with the Romanian government."

Well, we were encouraged. We explained about the embassy, and Bill advised us not to go.

"There is no way to go to the embassy," he said. "You go in there, you will never get out. You step inside, it is the end."

So we stay there a few days, then we call the embassy. They are very disappointed that we don't show up for the meeting.

"Well, we are concerned," I tell them. "That is Romanian territory and we are really not thinking about going home. Why don't we just meet each other somewhere else, in a little restaurant or a coffee bar, even on the street. I don't care. But we really wouldn't like to go to the embassy."

The guy we are talking to is just the typical embassy officer. "Listen, I'm telling you frankly," he says. "You better come. If not, forget it." And he bangs down the phone.

We went back to Bill Archer and told him the embassy is insisting. So he sent his personal secretary, a lawyer, and a United Nations representative with us, and we call the embassy and tell them we will be coming at 10 o'clock in the morning.

We walk into the embassy and we can see from their faces they are thinking: We got you. Then they notice the people with us and start to get a little nervous.

"Who they are?" they ask. We introduce them.

"No, we don't need them," they say. "They can't come in. They haven't been invited."

"They haven't been invited," we admit, "but they are protecting us on the part of the American government."

We could tell it was a confusional situation for them. They didn't know how to act. So they change the room, and ten minutes later the ambassador shows up.

He is very brief with us, very short, and he doesn't want to speak a word of English. Archer's people had told us to speak English as much as we could, so we could have witnesses who could intervene in case of any kind of conflict. So they are speaking Romanian and we were responding in our bad English. They say how twenty-one million people from Romania are crying. In the name of the president and the population they are asking us to say it was just a joke, and it will be no problem. We can go back and get everything back.

They couldn't believe we really wanted to stay in America. We had just built a new addition on our house. Everything we owned was there. Andrea was there. They did not understand that we would leave all that behind.

"How about the empty house?" I ask them. "How about everything that is already gone?"

"No problem," they say. "They are deposited in a good place. Don't worry about. Everything will be carried back."

"What about our positions?" I say. "We did not leave the country because we wanted to be rich, but because we wanted a fair professional situation."

"No problem," they say. "The federation will be directed to recognize the big mistakes they made, and you will be treated in the fairest way. The prime minister, who was supporting you guys so much, is sending his regards. Don't worry. Go back."

We explain that our decision is firm, and they changed their tone. They started to be nervous and nasty, and the talk was over. So there is no result, except that we gave them a written notice asking for our family reunification.

Then we went back to see Archer, and we were worried. We were afraid that we would not get Andrea out for years.

"Look," he told us, "I can't pick the phone up now, because it wouldn't be smart. So let's wait a few days, keep you guys around here, then call them again. If they don't give you any kind of answer, at that time I will step into the scene."

So we stayed for a while with Steve Gereben. Then we called the embassy.

"What the hell you want?" the guy asked me. "You were just here a week ago. Who told you to call, anyway? Go back home and see your daughter if you want."

So that was their response. There was no room for negotiation. We went back to see Bill Archer, and he got on the phone. "Look," he said, "I want to talk to the Romanian ambassador right now. I'm Bill Archer, and I have in my office three friends who have a concern. I just wanted to assure them that they'll get their daughter and that the other fellow will get his wife and child in twenty-four hours."

"Sure, sure," they tell him, "but you know, is not easy. It has to go through official channels, and the government has to sign in order to release. . . ."

"No," Archer said. "I want to have an answer in twenty-four hours about how the procedure is going to go."

"Sure," they tell him.

"It doesn't matter what answer they give," Archer tells us. "I'm here and I'm going to follow through."

So we go back to Los Angeles, and as the weeks pass and our situation does not improve, our physical and mental condition is very down. All I know is we have to get out of Los Angeles. There is no way to make it there.

Then one day I decide to call Paul Ziert, based on what he had told me a long time ago, which was that if I ever came to the United States and wanted to do some summer clinics, to call him up.

So I telephone to the University of Oklahoma and ask for Paul. "Hey, Bela," he says. "How you are doing?"

"Trying to learn English," I say. "Trying to make a living. It's pretty hard, though. Look, Paul, do you still have any interest in hiring? Anything is good for us."

He called back later and said that the university would have a position in the physical education department, starting the first of September. In a few weeks, Paul says, he can also offer us positions coaching in his summer camps.

"Fantastic, Paul," I say. "But I have no money to get there unless I am walking, and Oklahoma is a faraway place."

"Don't worry," he assures me. "These guys are serious and they will pay for your air fare."

In the meantime Geza, who is a very talented choreographer, is offered a job at a club in Sacramento. So for the first time since we walk out of that hotel in Manhattan, the possibilities are looking good for all of us.

When we go to Norman the university gives us a small apartment at no charge, and of the money we make, we spend only enough to eat. The rest, 99 percent of it, we put aside in order to build up some small capital. Because my previous bitter and hard experience showed me that there is no way in this country to succeed unless I stand on my own feet.

In Europe it is very different. The tradition there is that all the families support very strongly their members. If somebody gets in financial or legal trouble or any kind of bad situation, the whole family is standing behind, supporting the troubled person. They are taking care, pulling together. The family ties are so close. That is why there are family businesses and family professions and why nobody is going very far away, why they are not spreading out of the country. There is the old people's house, and the kids are living around, maybe even on the same street.

So it was hard for me to come to this country with no relatives here, and figure out how to make it. Here everybody is so independent and much cooler. There is not the strong family relations. The sentimental ties, they do not exist as much. The concept of the life is much more practical, with everybody going his own way. There is nothing you can get here for free. You cannot live based on somebody's goodwill.

"Oh, look at the poor man," they say in Europe. "He's in trouble. He is good guy, let's go help him. Let's give him a job. Even if he is just lazy, well, he might start working one of these days."

This cheap sentimentality, it does not work here in America. It is actually much more practical and healthy, this mentality, but for us it was like a shock.

"I would like you suckers to come here for just a year to try to make a living," I told some Romanian friends later. "You would consider a sanitorium in Siberia a holiday, like Hawaii."

The competition is so big here. You cannot count on somebody to recognize, yes, you are an outstanding person in your area, let me offer you a job. That does not exist here. The better you are in your profession, the more people would like to keep you back. It is a hard and cruel reality. So you've got to go and climb through all that mess all by yourself. That is why so many outstanding personalities from around the world, they come here and disappear. After years, nobody even knows them. You find them in a very small apartment somewhere, just taking their life from day to day. Because they never can find the moral strength to build up again here what they were once recognized and compensated for.

That is very hard to understand and hard to take. But the advantage is that America is still the country of the opportunities. If someone is persistent and able to make major personal sacrifices and works like crazy, you can take those opportunities and turn them to your benefit. That possibility, to build up in a short time a situation that is favorable to you and your family, is a great one, and it does not exist anywhere in Europe.

Yes, the competition exists here, but if you are taking the opportunity, working hard and are dedicated, you can make it, and soon you will not have to depend on anybody.

So we work hard in Oklahoma, saving every little penny. I work at a gymnastics club and a summer camp, and in the evenings I took whatever jobs I could.

The summer went by and we were on the same kind of strict and severe type of life—going to work, coming home, and reducing everything to the minimum expenditure. But at least we have jobs in the profession that we love. The only problem is Andrea. It is now late in August, and nothing has happened. Martha was at the end of her wits, very down. The embassy had said they needed one more personal meeting to have any kind of decision. We knew Bill Archer was helping, but we also realized that the Romanians were doing what they wanted. Nobody could force them.

Well, it happened that one of the summer camps I was working at was in Richmond, which is not too far from Washington. So we asked one of the gymnasts who had a car if he would drive us to Washington.

In the meantime we had called the embassy, and they were so-so, trying to tell nothing. So we realize there is nothing done, nothing to expect from them.

When we get to Washington, we prepare to try once more. We hadn't called Bill Archer, because we didn't want to abuse his time. But we happened to pass his office, and on a chance I pop my head in.

"Your daughter is not here yet?" Bill asks. "I thought she arrived a long time ago."

"No," I say. "I was embarrassed to ask."

"You didn't let me know?" he says, and he gets on the phone. "I want to speak to the ambassador," he begins. "Look, almost three months ago I was asking you to give me an answer in twenty-four hours. You said the process had been set in motion and it would only be a couple of weeks. It has been many weeks.

"Now, listen. I need not an answer, but a telephone call from the Romanian ambassador stating that the Karolyis' daughter is leaving the country in twenty-four hours. Because for a long time we have controversial news coming from your country, and stories of violations of human rights regarding family reunifications, a matter that I will suggest for discussion at the next committee meeting. That might have an effect on Romania's most-favored-nation status." Bang, he slams the phone down.

The next day I call Deva and talk to my father, who was all the time going back and forth to see what the situation was, and never getting any answer.

"Hey, what happened?" he asks me. "The chief of the police department yesterday called personally for me to go and pick up the passport for Andrea. He was so kind, all smiles. A few days earlier he almost kicked me out. What happened over there? This is crazy. She is free to go?"

"Don't worry about," I tell him. "Just put her on the airplane and have her come. Make the arrangements as fast as you can."

And on the seventh of September, just around ten days later, Andrea arrived in New York City. It was incredible. That little bug came off the big plane alone with a small travel bag, running past Customs, flying through to Martha who was running towards her. The Customs people are yelling, "Hey, what's going on?" But then they saw this unbelievable scene, mother and child crying and hugging. "Don't worry," they say, "we'll do it later."

So we go back to Oklahoma, where school starts a week later. Andrea doesn't know any English either, so we put her in second grade, one less than she had been in Romania. It was a good idea; she felt more comfortable. Still, it was a tough adjustment for her. She never complained, but sometimes going to bed there'd be tears in her eyes. "Nobody is talking to me," she would say. "No friends." Her little heart was hurt. But that didn't last too long.

So now we have reached our first goal—Andrea is with us. The second step was to build up our life to give her the chance to be like any other child, without the stress of living day-to-day.

Before she came we were fighting for our existence, to make for her a nice situation. I was working day and night to buy some furniture, and to have a little bed ready for her when she arrived. Now we wanted to establish ourselves in our profession. We were grateful to Paul Ziert for what he had done for us, but we wanted to have our own program. So in the fall of 1981 I began to look for a possibility to establish our program.

In December some people from Houston who knew Bill Archer came to Norman, and talked about having us come down there, where they say they own a couple of gyms. They invite us to come down at Christmastime to do a clinic and see the facility, to have an idea of what is going on. They present this one gym, about twenty miles northwest of the city, as a place where they are going to put up a powerful training center, with us in charge.

At the time we don't know that they don't own the gym, that they just have the intention of buying it, but it is all right with us. The gym wasn't anything really impressive, but we thought it would be a good first step for us to be in a position to start something exactly according to our minds and knowledge. So as soon as we finalized an arrangement in January of 1982, we began getting ready to move. And in February, a month that most big changes in my life have happened, we went down to Houston and began to work.

We had three other partners, but mostly they were involved in other businesses too. The gymnasium was merely an investment for them. The only persons actually related to the instruction were us. Right away we start to organize a small program, to develop our first American generation. We pull the kids tighter together, we raise the intensity of the preparation, and pretty soon we put together a small team, just from the local kids. Our time before the state championships is not very much, but we knew it would be important to show a good shape and a new trend.

Well, we won the Texas Class I title right away. We went to Nationals, and for the first time a kid from here, Paige Spiller, becomes champion on the vault. It produced a sensation. In a few months many kids asked to come down and train with us. So that was our first professional satisfaction in this country.

On the business side, though, things were not going too good. The partners find it hard to run efficiently their additional gym, and when new financial difficulties came up, they suddenly got into conflict.

It was hard to get through the summer with enough students to generate sufficient income to make the business go decently and catch up with back payments and unpaid loans. Summer is a bad time for gymnastics, anyway, because the students are taking vacation and doing other activities. By September the partners decide to sell, and they told us, well, here is the situation.

"Okay," I say, "but as partners we have first option to buy." We established $40,000 as the price of the business. Now, Martha and I had managed to save $10,000 and we borrowed $20,000 more and bought out the other guys.

Many people said it was the dumbest thing that somebody can do, but we knew it was now or who knows when. So we took the chance and the challenge.

I didn't know much English or specifics about running a small business in America. But I had the knowledge of running a gymnastics program. As for the business part of it, I relied on my feeling for it, my instinct. If it makes sense to me, I thought, let's do it.

Our problem, though, was that in October we had only 86 students. Can you imagine what kind of income can generate 86 students? So first we announced politely that everybody that used to be hired in this gym, unfortunately, we cannot keep. There is simply no way to pay anybody. So we take on everything ourselves—instruction, administration, secretarial work, cleaning. Everything. We are teaching classes from early morning to late evening. And sometimes I am staying there until early morning, trying to put the gym in better shape, to give it a better aspect and make it pleasant.

After a while the people who had been coming here a long time were very positively surprised. People who were used to dusty, dirty, miserable conditions now have a nicer environment. They see that everything is clean and bright and smells normal. The toilets and bathrooms are shiny, and mirrors are on the walls. We put up a few pictures and posters to make the building look like a gymnasium, not a barn.

Well, without any special advertising, with word just going from people to people, our program started to grow relatively fast. By January we had grown from 86 to 168 students. We were paying off our back debts. And we were beginning to look towards 1984 and the Olympic Games with a very fine gymnast named Dianne Durham.

She had come from Gary, Indiana, and was the first girl from outside the local area who moved down to train with us. Her mother had called us in Oklahoma, asking if we could take her then, but we had no way to give her the opportunity to train efficiently. But as soon as we came to Houston we called her and said okay, and she came right down. We had no idea that black kids had never done well in American gymnastics. We only knew that she had great strength and speed and confidence, and we begin to work intensively with her.

In four months she wins the national junior elite title. Then, at Fort Worth in June, Dianne shares the all-around championship with Kathy Johnson at the U.S.G.F. international invitation meet.

Texas had never had great gymnastics. But when we started to produce, the people here appreciated it. In their general manner Texans are proud people, and they try to have outstanding things going on. This was a positive factor for us, and we felt immediately the support. The Chamber of Commerce would call up, people would congratulate us. It made us have the feeling of belongness, which was important.

In only a few months everyone knows the Sundance Gym and the Sundance Kids. We are dominating Texas, and Dianne is becoming the best gymnast in the country. And before long comes a relatively unknown gymnast to train with us. A powerful little girl from a coal-miner area of West Virginia whose name is Mary Lou Retton.

7

MARY LOU
That Big Leap

My first workout at Karolyi's was on a Sunday afternoon, and that's always the toughest of the week. I started on bars, and Bela had me doing new skills right away, things I'd never even tried that the other girls had already been working on. Well, I was trying my hardest to impress everybody, and I was just killing myself, falling and bruising things but also making improvement. I wasn't going to cry and show Bela I was a baby, but it was so hard.

What made it even worse was that I couldn't figure out what Bela was telling me, because his accent was so heavy. He'd say something and I'd look at Dianne Durham or Beth Pope. "What'd he say, what'd he say?" I'd ask them.

When I got back after that first day I was sore and confused and wondering what I'd gotten myself into. My God, I thought, is it going to be like this every day?

All of it was totally new to me. The intensity of the workout, having all the girls screaming and pushing for each other, made me feel like I was part of a team, and I liked that. But I wasn't used to going full-out for three hours, with somebody watching me every second, and it took me a while to adjust to that.

From that first day Bela changed everything I'd been doing for eight years, from the way I tumbled to what I ate. I'm always going to have to watch my weight. Because of my build it'll be a lifetime thing for me.

Back in West Virginia I'd never thought my weight was a problem. I was pretty close to one hundred pounds, but Gary Rafaloski had never said anything about it. But the first thing Bela said to the Spillers was, "Put her on a diet."

I used to eat anything—sandwiches, sweets, whatever. My mom is a great cook and she used to pile on all this stuff so it was hanging off the edges of the plate. When I first moved in with the Spillers, I was a little bit uneasy, so I'd just put a little on my plate.

But eventually I really did change the way I ate. I began to eat chicken—I love chicken, I could live on it. I'd have fish, lots of salads, and fruits and vegetables.

Once I began watching my weight I realized that the extra four or five pounds made such a difference on me. It wasn't that I'd been fat, but I didn't look as good. When I got down around ninety-four it made me look much more streamlined, and I felt better, too.

But the biggest adjustments I had to make were in intensity and technique. Back in Fairmont, where the workouts were two hours, I used to go full-out, but it wasn't full-out enough. I'd do one or two bar routines. "That's good," I'd tell myself. "My hands are a little red. Let's stop." In Houston I had to do them five, six, seven, eight times, and doing it 98 percent wasn't good enough. Bela wanted 102 percent, and he wanted it every time.

That's what makes the difference between a good gymnast and a great one, but I'd never realized that until I went to Karolyi's. In Houston I'd do a bars routine and land on my feet and go, "Yeah!" but Bela would be shaking his head, "No, no, no."

"Well," I'd say to myself, frustrated, "it was good in West Virginia."

I had to forget everything I'd learned since childhood, because everything was opposite now. I'd developed all these bad habits, which I didn't know were bad habits, and they were difficult to break. After you've been doing something in a certain way for six years your body is used to it and you can't change overnight.

77

Tumbling, for example. I'd take off with my head down, but it was supposed to be up, which is only logical, because it helps your rotation. Vault was my best event, yet it was all wrong. I had this natural explosiveness, and I used to run with short, choppy steps, and just go crazy.

So Bela changed it all—my running, my techniques, my arm style, my head. I'd thought my performance level on bars was medium. I was doing a difficult routine, but it wasn't clean. My legs were bent and I was generally sloppy. I'd just go through it, get it done. Well, Bela got on me about extension and toes, which he wanted pointed. He didn't want just a little swing, he wanted it bigger and bigger. He wanted perfection, and I was far from perfect, especially on the beam.

When I went to Houston I had the reputation of always having at least one or two falls. Back home if I stayed on for a whole routine, it was a miracle. I'd be waving and smiling. Bela told me how he'd talked to Martha after seeing me perform in Utah. "Look how powerful this girl is," he'd told her. "But she can't even stay on the beam," Martha said. "No, Bela, no."

So I was her project. Bela gets all the strong ones who can tumble and vault. Martha gets all us uncoordinated types on the beam. That's the hardest job because it takes a lot of patience to get somebody confident and consistent up there.

But both Nadia and Ecaterina Szabo were both great beamers, just like all the Romanian girls were, and Martha had taught them all. "What makes them so good?" I'd ask her. "Because they learn to walk on the beam right," she'd tell me. "They turn their feet out." Mine turned in. I think I'm pigeon-toed, and it's hard to be a great beamer when your feet don't naturally turn the right way.

I had other problems, though. I'd fallen so often in the past that I'd go on knowing I was going to fall. I'd feel myself wobble a little and think, Here it comes. Get ready. Here it comes. So I'd fall. It was a matter of not being prepared physically or mentally for the beam. I also wasn't used to being watched. In Fairmont I'd do beam by myself. "So what?" I'd say, when I fell. "They didn't see me." But Martha was eagle-eyed, watching every move.

I couldn't goof off, I really couldn't, because they saw everything.

And that's good, because when you get into a competition, so do the judges.

But I wasn't used to that at all. I was accustomed to getting through workouts without worrying about the technique and the polishing, and that's why I was so sloppy—in Bela's mind, anyway.

"No, not good," he'd tell me after a routine. "Not good."

Gosh, it was *supposed* to be good, I'd think. What do I have to do to make him say "good"?

I had a lot of adjustments to make those first few weeks—to a new family, a new school, a new city, new friends, a new gym, and new training techniques. But the biggest adjustment was to Bela.

I was a little intimidated by him at first, because I'd heard all these mysterious rumors and didn't know if they were true. I found out he was really warm and nice once you got to know him, but I couldn't even understand what he meant that first week or two.

"Grrrowwwlll," he'd say, and I'd wonder, What's he saying? It took me a while to figure out his mumbles and his grunts and his growls and his ahas. But I realized pretty quickly that our personalities had a lot in common. We're both pretty open, and it's not hard to tell how we're feeling just by looking at us.

"Ohh, I hate the ones with the long face," Bela would tell me. "You cannot tell what they are thinking. I always tried to get Nadia to smile. Smile, Nadia, smile, smile, I'd say." But he said that just wasn't the way she was. But with me you could always tell what I was thinking just by looking at my face. I can't hold it in. I'd come in some days when the last thing I wanted to do was work out, and Bela would see that and start making jokes, massaging my shoulders and getting me pumped up.

He'd call me "Booboolina," which means fat, and it would get me so mad. "Okay, Boo-boo," he'd say, and begin to laugh. So our personalities pretty well clicked, but that didn't make workouts any easier.

I'd do a routine I thought was good and I'd land it and grin and he'd give me the shake of the head. "No, no, no," he'd say, and then tell me what was wrong.

It was so frustrating because it felt good to me, but it just wasn't good enough for him. It just killed me. I wasn't swinging high enough or wasn't pointing enough or whatever, and I knew he was right. Still, it took me a couple of months to realize that it might feel good but it wasn't great. It was great back in West Virginia, I'd think. But now I come here and it's only so-so.

Everything was different than it had been in West Virginia. Back there I'd hurt myself, and they'd say, "Oh, you banged a finger, go sit down." Here it was "so what?" You keep going. You show your hurt finger to Bela. "Oh, yes," he says. "Let's do another one." I was in shape in West Virginia. So why am I so sore here? I'd wonder.

So I think the Spillers were curious to see how I'd react to Bela and his workouts. It probably took me only a couple of weeks to start yelling and screaming about him in the house.

"My head is *up*," I'd shout, "I *know* it's up."

"It'll take time," Mr. Spiller told me.

"I know," I'd say, "but he still keeps telling me.

I'd be mad, but I'd be laughing at the same time, and I guess they were amused by it all. The Spillers really helped out a lot. My parents went back to Fairmont after the first few days, but the Spillers became just like my parents, and they gave me that family atmosphere that was so important.

Houston was just so different from Fairmont. Fairmont is twenty-five thousand people, and there's not much to do. You hang out at McDonald's. Houston is three million people, huge and growing every day, and the pace is so much faster. The people talk differently, the climate is different, everything. No mountains, no snow, all that humidity. I really missed the snow. In Fairmont there are hills and mountains all around. We have this huge driveway in front of our house, and when it iced over we'd go sledding on it.

But the Spillers made me feel right at home, so I was pretty lucky with the homesick part. After workout I could go home and be with a family. The Spillers had taken in other gymnasts before, so they were used to having new girls around. That made it an easy transition for me. It took no time at all.

They had a boy named Perry who was Ronnie's age. There was another one, Preston, who was three years younger than Perry. Then there was Paige, who was a year younger than me, and Patrick, the little one. Paige and I became like sisters. She was a great vaulter who'd won the national Class I championship, and we even had pretty much the same build—short, muscular legs, very strong. We'd talk a lot—about Bela, about workouts, school, all sorts of things. She didn't have an older sister, and I didn't have a younger one. And I'd never had a younger brother who'd get in your room, mess around with your stuff. It only took me about a week to start fighting with Patrick.

Sometimes I'd get lonely for home. When I'd get down in the dumps I'd call and say, "Ohh, I miss you, I miss you." My mom would write me every single day, sending me a dollar for lunch money and telling me everything that happened. "I'm baking a cake right now," she'd say. It gave me a taste of home, and I looked forward to those letters.

At the beginning my Fairmont friends and I wrote letters a lot and even called each other, but that started slacking off. I expected that. They have their lives to live and I have mine, so it didn't really hurt me when they stopped writing. I was making new friends here, too.

I'd enrolled at Northland Christian, a private school not far from Karolyi's gym, where Paige was. It was a little scary at first, but I'm not one to hold back. I just go out and make friends. "Hi, I'm Mary Lou," I'll say. "Who are you?" So I had no problem at school.

Before long I was feeling more comfortable in the gym, too. People don't realize what a major change it is to move from one gym to another. Just the difference in atmosphere and how the place is laid out. When you're on bars or beam, there are spots you look for on the ceiling to keep your bearings when you're in the air. When I went to Karolyi's, all of them were new.

It took a while for my body to get used to Bela's workouts, too. Most gymnasts work hard during the week, then take weekends off. But Bela's hardest workout is on Sunday, which makes sense, because when we have to perform we're used to being out there then. Other girls, who don't work that day, wonder, Why are we here?

Three days a week we'd have double workouts, one in the morning, another at night. At first it was hard to get moving at 8 o'clock, to

81

get up on a four-inch balance beam and make your body function. But when you come back at night, you still feel stretched out and it's easier to go.

After doing it for a while your body gets used to that cycle. It can almost tell you what day it is. And after a few weeks of Bela's workouts, of Martha working me on the beam, I could feel my body changing. I'd lost those extra pounds and gotten trimmer. I'm strong enough that I can carry that weight, and I have no problem working out with it, but it's so much easier when it's off. So I could feel myself getting stronger. My definition was better, I just felt good. I'd still get sore, but that meant I was getting the workouts I needed and that made me happy.

I was getting used to Bela and his idea of perfection, too. I'd finally realized that you had to give him the best, more than better. I'd do a routine with a little mistake in it, look at him when it was done and say, "Let me do it again." I knew what it took to make him say "good." Sometimes it took five or six repetitions to get it right. "Good," he'd say. "Good. Let's do one more. Just one more." After a couple of weeks I realized that when Bela said "Just one more," we were in the middle of the workout.

The whole idea was to get a routine so that it was good enough for Bela, because if it was, it would be good enough for anybody. But I've seen girls who said, "I don't care what he thinks. It feels good. I'm doing it this way." And they got no better. They stayed at the same level. You have to make that big leap, and it can be frustrating, because you go through this period of time where you try so hard but things just don't go. Finally, though, it starts coming. You've just got to get yourself through that hard time.

Some girls won't do that, and some will. But I had to, and I did. After I was at Bela's a couple of months I was improving and I could sense it. I'd also figured out how to deal with Bela. There were times when I'd come into the gym and see it right in his eyes. "Oh, gosh," I'd tell myself. "Don't mess with him tonight."

Seeing sloppiness or the same mistakes over and over again drives him crazy. He'll frown and the mustache will droop and his eyes will flash. "I don't know what you're doing," he'll growl. "You've lost your mind. I don't know."

Once he got disgusted and said that we weren't training for the championships of 1984. "You're training for flea market contest of 1960 on the corner of Bamwood Street," he'd say. He was steaming, but I just burst out laughing. I turned my back and just went "phfffftttt," and he sort of cracked a smile.

But once, after I'd been there a couple of months, we had this terrible scene. We were working out on bars, and an ABC film crew was there watching.

I'd chalked up, and everything was going all right. I was doing a free hip circle on the low bar, and then my hands slipped off and I landed on my chin and ripped open that little piece of skin between my lower lip and my gum. I was horrified. I'm like, "Ooohhh," with this big hole in my mouth and blood running down my chin, and ABC's right in my face getting it all.

Well, Bela comes right over and he looks mad. "Get up, get up," he barks. "Go. Go to the bathroom, get out of here." I was stunned. That was the first time he'd ever yelled at me.

It was awful. They took me to the emergency room at the hospital, but they couldn't put stitches in it. They couldn't do anything with it. My mouth was all swollen; I couldn't open it. I went home crying, and that night Bela called me up and he yelled at me.

"I cannot believe you," he says. "With ABC there, you made such a big scandal, like a baby. Don't ever do this again. You got to be a strong athlete, not a scared rabbit."

Well, I was packed, ready to go back to Fairmont. I'd been depressed before, usually when a workout hadn't gone well. "Don't make any rash decisions," my parents would tell me when I phoned. "Talk things over. You've come this far, you can't quit now."

This time, though, was different. "I'm ready to come home," I told my mom. "I don't know if I can take this." I didn't go to school the next day. I mean, I could barely talk.

All of a sudden, the doorbell rings and in walks Bela. Oh, God, I think. What now?

"Oh, honey," he says, giving me a big hug with this apologetic look on his face. "Oh, I am so sorry." And, of course, everything was fine. Bela was just so scared seeing that big hole in my mouth and all the blood that his first reaction was to get angry.

At that point nothing was going to make me go home. I was improving every day. I'd gotten my techniques right, and I was excited about it. "I'm learning this, I'm learning that," I'd say when I called home. And it was such a great feeling to be part of a team.

Just two weeks after I got to Houston we had gone up to the Olympic Training Center in Colorado Springs for the American Classic, which was a qualifying meet for the championships of the U.S.A. We came in wearing our warmups, these real pretty white satin jackets that say "Karolyi's" on the back, and we're all confident and people just stop and look at us. It's not like we're cocky or anything, but everybody knows that Bela trains us well, that we're not going to be messing up.

Other teams, you can see in their workouts, in their competitive routines, that they're just not ready, they're not sure. You can see it in their faces before they go out. You can tell from their thirty-second warmup. They get up and they're doing parts, and we're throwing routine after routine.

We know we're on a roll. When you see your teammate doing well you want to do even better, and it just keeps going. It even happens in practice. Someone goes up and does a trick and you want to improve on it. It's like you have judges every day.

Well, I could feel the difference in my abilities at that first meet at Colorado Springs. I was much stronger technically, just from being watched and corrected and made to do things over. I got my first perfect 10 in the vault there, and that helped me win the all-around after being seventh after the first day.

My style had already changed after only two weeks with Bela. Where I used to just run down on the vault and punch off, I'd circle my arms before I hit the board. And my head *was* up.

But my biggest improvement was on beam, where Martha had really been working me hard. When I first got to Houston I was falling off all the time. So much of it was mental, I finally realized.

If you think, God, I'm so scared, I know I'm going to fall, most likely you will. But over a period of time I started staying on and feeling good about it. I was a hard worker, and I think Martha could tell that I really wanted to be changed, that I wanted her help.

One thing that made a difference was not doing the roundoff layout. I was so inconsistent at it that I'd fallen off almost every competition. So the first thing Bela and Martha did was take it out and put an easier skill in, at least for the time being. So I was able to stay on and build up my consistency.

And gradually I stopped hearing the "no-no-nos" from Bela, and started getting "guuuds" and "behterrs." A lot of that was because I'd improved so much technically. But having Dianne Durham to compete against every day made a big difference, too.

Dianne was the first national-class gymnast to sign up with Bela, and there was no question that she was the top girl in the gym when I got there. But I started going, and Dianne saw me and she started going, and it was back and forth every day.

I guess we never let each other know that we were after one another, but it was head-on all the time. We were just so much alike. We were both more stocky than we were tall. I was less than five months older than she was, and we both had the same strengths and weaknesses. We were both just so solid and ready, and in competitions we would just kill everybody on optionals. When we went to Colorado Springs for the American Classic, I beat her in all-around, and in the floor final. And she beat me in the vault final.

It was obvious to me that it would be that way right up to the Olympic trials. I'd beat her, she'd beat me, I'd beat her. That's exactly what I'd needed for so long back in Fairmont, and what I hadn't been getting.

It's important to have somebody who's at your level going through the same thing you are every day.

"I'm tired today," you say.

"So am I," she says.

"My hands hurt today," you say.

"So do mine," she says.

So you realize you're not the only one suffering. That was really important when Martha would be watching you both like a hawk on beam, and Bela would be growling.

Once I'd hurt my wrist and Dianne had hurt her knee and neither of us could work out. So Bela told us both to jog about two or three miles outdoors. We *were* jogging, but he wouldn't believe us, so he made us run around the gym fifty times as punishment. That made both of us angry, so we had something else in common.

That was how it was all winter, every day in practice. It wasn't just a workout, it was the Olympic trials. But it wasn't only Dianne I had to be worried about. There were girls training in Oregon and Huntington Beach and Allentown, and some of them, like Kathy Johnson and Julianne McNamara and Tracee Talavera, had a lot more experience than I did.

They were all older than I was, had all been on the 1980 Olympic team, and all won medals at the world championships. I'd been reading about them and seeing their pictures in *International Gymnast* for years, but I hadn't been able to compete against them because I wasn't in their age group. Now I was.

From watching Tracee and Julianne on television I knew they were both very good on bars and beam—they had the long limbs for that. But what they were doing for vaults in competitions I was doing in warmups, and I thought I could outdo them in tumbling. So I was determined to keep my beam and bars up and keep progressing, because I knew I could compete with them. I just didn't know when I would have the chance.

They hadn't been at the American Classic when I'd won the all-around, but they were both at the Caesar's Palace Invitational in Las Vegas a little while later, and I beat them, winning both the all-around and the vault final. Well, that was a big, big deal for me. I went back to Houston and thought, Hey, I won. I beat Tracee Talavera and Julianne McNamara, the ones I see on TV.

That proved to me that my parents and I had made the right decision when I'd left home. Every time I called them now it was with good news, so whatever homesickness I still had just disappeared. I've always been an optimistic sort of person, anyway. If I get depressed

I rarely stay that way for very long. The only thing that really bothered me was having a bad workout, but I always knew I could come back that night or the next day and have a good one.

Well, within two months of arriving at Karolyi's I'd shown myself that I could beat anyone at the national level. But I still knew I had room for improvement. What I had to do now was make the breakthrough, to get to the point where my name was known in the international gymnastics community. People outside the sport don't realize how important that is.

If you're a well-known gymnast the judges expect something good from you, and even if it's not there they're still going to give you a decent score. If you don't have that name it's much easier for the judges to brush you aside with 9.3s and 9.4s because nobody expects much from you to begin with.

So making a reputation is important for a younger gymnast, and it's especially tough if there are a number of experienced girls on the scene. Because of the 1980 boycott it was even more difficult than usual to get named to the American team for the big international competitions. The best girls all stuck around for another four years.

Kathy Johnson had been on the national team for eight years and competed in four world championships. Tracee had been U.S. champion for the last two years, and Julianne was right behind her. All of them were shooting for the same thing I was—the 1984 Games. For the major international meets, which is where you get yourself seen by the people that matter, the gymnastics federation takes the top two Americans. Unless I could crack the Tracee-and-Julianne thing, I was going to be an alternate.

I'd beaten them once, but that didn't mean much. They might have had a bad day, I might have had a good one. People could look at it as a fluke. I had to beat them someplace where the Americans, Russians, Romanians, and everybody else were competing—like the American Cup, which was going to be in New York that year. That would be my breakthrough.

8

BELA

Something Fantastic

The first time I saw Mary Lou was at the junior national championship in Salt Lake City in the middle of 1982. Martha and I were standing on the bleachers, and we saw this little bug jumping around and laughing, very loud.

"Listen," I said to Martha, "that little sucker could be one of these days a big gymnast."

"Are you crazy?" Martha told me. "She is jumping ten times off of the beam. She is the most unconsistent kid I have ever seen in my life."

"Well," I said, "consistency can come with hard work, but the personality is hard to replace. This kid has got the spirit, got the guts. She can become aggressive."

At this time Mary Lou wasn't an aggressive performer. She was tumbling around, having good time. But I figure, yes, there is a spark somewhere in her eye, which I think can be turned into an aggressive style—to make her bite, to want to win, to build up the willingness to be the best.

Well, we meet her one more time just before Christmas in a special single-elimination tournament in Reno, Nevada. Her parents were there, but I didn't know who they were. Then her father stopped me and asked a few questions.

"Who is your daughter?" I said.

"Mary Lou."

"Oh, the little one. Sure, she's got tremendous physical potential, but she has to go a long way through hard work to turn into a great performer."

Then he mentioned that they might consider to send her down and train in Houston if there was a possibility. This was a little bit surprising to me, but I didn't refuse because I already had it in my mind. It was pleasant news to me that Mary Lou had the idea to come down, that she had the desire and the dedication. That made me even more sure, yes, she got the guts. She wants to be something and she's taking the challenge, taking the sacrifice to go away from home and come down to us.

"Certainly," I told Mr. Retton. "I am going to check back. And if I can work out something with housing and everything else, I am going to let you know."

So when I got back to Houston I asked around, and the Spiller family said, yes, if I consider that Mary Lou needed a place there, that their house was open for her. So I called Mary Lou's father, and in a few days they came down, visited the family, made the arrangements, and worked out the details with the school.

At that time I didn't know about her background. Later I found out that Mary Lou's father and grandfather were both in the coal-miner business, and that made me even more sympathetic.

Later, after the Olympic Games, I was invited to be part of the celebration that her little town put together, and it was a great pleasure for me. I felt like I was back home, because the miners are special personalities. They are very grateful for everything what happened, and I felt very good being there. They were such natural guys. "Let's go and have some schnapps," they say. That was how it used to be in Transylvania, and the influence of the surrounding medium all the time you can see on the kids. The desire. The fight. The feeling of, sure, I'm gonna do it.

Coal-miner kids everywhere are the same. They are used to difficulties, are used to struggle to make a living. They can understand having to put hard work in order to make it, and they are really appreciating when they get recognitions for it. It is not accidentally that those kids are all the time the most successful ones.

When Mary Lou first comes to us, though, I am not aware of all of this. I could see in Utah that the kid was strong, exploding. The floor was cracking under her. No question in my mind, Mary Lou was first-class material. But I wondered whether she could get her bubbling personality under control, because it is hard to get these explosive persons to be consistent.

I am sure in those first few weeks it was frustrating for her, because she had been the idol in West Virginia. But when she arrived in our gymnasium she wasn't even number two. Both Dianne Durham and Beth Pope were better, and on certain events several other kids were more consistent performers than Mary Lou was.

So that was my question. She is beautiful, open personality. But is she a strong person? Is she a fighter? I realized after a few days of workouts that she was, without question.

For gymnasts coming to our place from a loose program, the adjustment is horrible hard. They are used to having friends and joking partners around, but they find a very intensive environment. I am pushing them, and nobody even talks to anyone. There is great physical and mental fatigue from doing skills and routines hundreds of times. Some kids cannot do that, and they quit.

That is why I was watching Mary Lou very closely. I knew that every single muscle in that poor little body of hers was sore. I saw the tears and desperation in her eyes, looking so empty, and I knew she was in the balance to give up or not.

But she was still working and trying, looking at me and listening to me, wanting to do things properly. Mary Lou is an ambitious kid, and when people were doing better than she was, I could see the determination in her eyes. She is not giving up easy. Mary Lou is not the kind of person who makes hystericals. All the time I was pushing, pushing, pushing.

"How about going one more time?" I would say. And her response was all the time yes. Sure I will.

"Every time you say, 'That's the last one,' " she would say to me, "we know very well there's going to be around fifty more."

That was my purpose, to say always, "One more time. One more time. Last time. Then, one more time." Just to see if she would do it one more time. And she always did.

"Well," I told myself. "That is a good sign. She never showed that she might give up."

After a while you would not believe the personality changes Mary Lou went through, from an excitable kid to someone who becomes step by step more intent. She got so excited about her progress that she was picking up technical corrections and new skills right away. Mary Lou is a tremendously positive person. Her personality was a craziness, but the excitement and the fun is radiating all the time. She was so happy when she did something well that it generated a much easier adjustment for her. At the same time it made it a great pleasure for us to work with her. Mary Lou was so open, all eyes and ears, picking up everything, and her willingness to be better transformed her.

Her biggest problem was to make her have patience and consistency, to have her hitting, hitting, hitting the same routines, repeating the same thing, which is sometimes very boring. It is not her style to spend too much time with one thing; Mary Lou liked to jump from one thing to another. After a few weeks, though, her determination and capacity for fantastic hard work made Mary Lou pass everybody in the gym except one—Dianne Durham.

Dianne was the main obstacle to her being the best athlete in our program, and it set up an unbelievable competitive situation. I had not prepared Dianne for Mary Lou's arrival. Let the situation continue rolling, I thought. The stronger will be the better. Well, very quickly it became a great spectacle, each of them pushing the other one—Dianne, Mary Lou, Dianne, Mary Lou, every day, every night. All those hidden psychological ambitions, the physical abilities, the competitive spirits and, yes, the jealousies.

It wasn't a friendly competition, it was aggressive. I could see it in workouts. When one would do a new trick, the other one was dying.

But the next workout you could bet your life that the other one would try to do it. That was how Nadia and Teodora Ungureanu had pushed each other ten years earlier in Romania. Two great kids, exactly like Dianne and Mary Lou, and nobody knew which one is the better one.

It was life or death competition, week after week, and it was tremendously positive for both of them, even though I doubt that they recognized it. But Martha and I recognized it immediately as coaches.

Fortunately, both girls had the same body type, the same drive, and they were both good in the same events. So the competition was even. Of course, we try to make the best advantage out of this, and I was tough with them, never letting them take it easy. Sometimes, you know, they would make a little coalition figuring that if both of them are slowing down a little, I could not say nothing.

But they could not do that indefinitely because one didn't want to slow down while the other one was working hard. Still, one day I am on to their little game. "Hey, you get out," I say. "Both of you. Out from the gym. I am not wasting time with you."

Ahh, they get mad. Ooohh, such bad faces. They were standing outside and they were ready to give up, both of them. So I give a little speech, to Mary Lou especially.

"The way to get to the fame and glory is a hard way," I tell her. "Not easy. Does not happen from one day to the other. It takes a long time, consistent work."

"Well," Mary Lou says, "last week . . . ."

"Yes," I say, "last week. But what about this week? Every week, every day, every workout gotta be taken with the same dedication. We don't want to destroy what we builded up so hard for months. We don't want to have a sloppy and uncontrolled situation. And most of all, we don't want to have you injured. We want you to build up nicely, to perform correctly and safely."

"Well, but Dianne," she says. "What are you going to say to her?"

"Don't worry about Dianne," I say. "I am going to have discussion with Dianne, too." And I do.

Most days, though, those two are working unbelievable hard. And before long it is absolutely clear to me that they have a great possibility not only to make the Olympic team, but to win individual medals, which no American girls have ever done.

For many years this was a mystery to me, because from the first time I came here for an exhibition tour in 1971, I was shocked by how many talented kids the United States had lined up. My God, I thought, these kids are coming and killing us. They were performing skills beautifully, with so much raw physical ability. I went home and made a big report to the Romanian federation.

"Hey, listen," I said. "Our number-one contenders for the 1972 Olympic Games won't be the Russians, but the Americans. It's unbelievable what they're producing. There'll be no way to beat them."

When we came back in 1972 we beat them by several points, but still the feeling was, this is the last time. Every time I came to this country I got the same sensation—is the end, the last time we can beat the Americans. But we always did, year after year.

I was amazed, wondering what the hell is going on here? I never could understand—until I got here. Then I saw how the whole preparation is covered with ignorance, with people taking the easy way. It wasn't a question of technique, because the American kids came out with good skills. But they were not prepared properly physically or mentally to have the endurance that produces consistency, which is necessary for a major four-day competition like a world championship or an Olympic Games.

The physical preparation, to make the kids fit and strong, was ignored, and the mental aspect was blocked. So the willingness of the gymnast to go out and show, to justify the reason for the hard work with a result, never happened. You wanted to ask the parents, if you are paying so much money, why not let the kid go out and work hard? But if you are a coach talking that way, you have to be willing to stand behind the kid and spend your time, too.

There is also the question of liabilities, of being willing to take the risk of the child being injured. Sure, these things are existing, but you've got to take the chance. If you don't, you never can do it. So the easy way is, don't do it. Forget it. And that mentality was reinforced by the leading personalities in gymnastics here.

Later they came up with the convenient ideology, saying that the

Russians and East Germans and Romanians are using methods which can never work in this country. They talked about the miraculous, mystical way the eastern Europeans prepared their gymnasts. Tormenting, starving, torturing, with so many scientists standing behind them.

"But look at us," they say. "We are not helped from the government, so obviously we cannot do it."

Nobody ever said, we cannot do it because we are lazy. We do not want to take the hard way and make sacrifices. So it was easy to promote this indolence. It was easy to float with the river. And that is why they never did anything in women's gymnastics.

We saw that same attitude when we came to live in this country. American coaches were saying in the newspapers that the Karolyis' kingdom was over, that this wasn't like Romania where the government is paying. And that the American kids are spoiled, that they do not want to work. But I knew that kids are kids anywhere in the world. You can go in Alaska or Africa or Arabia, the kids are going to be the same anyplace, with their good parts, their bad parts, their ambitions and dreams. If strongly they are guided they can produce unbelievable results. So that was our approach in Houston, just as it was in Transylvania.

And there is reciprocal respect. We respect them, but we also strongly ask them to respect us. Sometimes because the kids are paying, the coaches are playing the clown for them. Not in our gym. We have the same organization, the same discipline, the same intensity in our workouts. And we have the same goal—to produce lionesses, not scared rabbits.

I have always been a competitive person and I try to influence the kids the same way. When you go to a competition, I tell them, you go to win, not just to be there. Your performance is the most important thing. Everything else has to be excluded. So don't look at the others. Don't distract your attention from the objective.

So very seldom in our lives do we have disappointing performances in competitions. Not all of our gymnasts were world-class level, but all of them were fighters and always did better than expected, going through the difficulties, never giving up. That was our belief—in no situation give up. Seriously, honestly, finish the competition, good or bad. Make an honorable presence. Make yourself look like an athlete, not a fool or a clown.

So we never allow scenes. Our girls will be falling, spraining ankles and elbows, bruising themselves. The tears are going, but there are no scandals, no hystericals. "Don't make yourself somebody to feel sorry for," we tell our girls. "Make the people to appreciate you as a strong person, even in a bad situation. Not to say, oh, poor child."

All these things we are transmitting and translating constantly during workouts. It is not something we are introducing for half an hour. Is not a lesson, is not a skill. It is builded up through a long period of time. These things are creating strong personalities, fighters. You look around and what catches your attention is the desire in the eyes, how they are taking the risk. They are playing with their lives, no question about it.

If they're sloppy, if they fall, the accident is there. We don't want accidents. We don't want to cripple somebody. We want to build good, powerful athletes.

It is no coincidence that our gymnasts have also been good students, and the reason is simple. They have less time, so they have to organize it. They are practical, quick, directed, and that is why they are learning faster. Those other kids who are having all day long, sure, they take their time. And when the evening comes they are tired from some dumb thing and they say, ahh, tomorrow. So they delay, and they grow up as sloppy, ignorant persons.

All of our girls finished college in Romania and came out as eminent people. Doctors, civil engineers, almost all of them in leading positions, resolving their problems quickly and efficiently. The American girls, they are no different, and in a very short time we were making rapid progress. Our program was growing, too, mostly by word of mouth.

In October of 1982 when we took over the club we had 86 students. By January the number had grown to 168, and by the end of the winter it was 250. In the meantime we didn't hire nobody and didn't take any salaries, either, because we were paying all the back debts. But by 1983, even though we have no penny in our pocket, we were clean. There were no liabilities on our head. So we own the business, but we have no equipment of our own. We had leased it from another company. But we were finally in a position where we could ask for a loan from the Texas Commerce Bank.

One day I just walked in and talked to the president of the branch nearby. He was a nice person and very interested to view our place. Well, when he came by and saw what are now four hundred children in the gym and the enthusiasm and the feverish activity that was going on, he was very impressed. "Yes," he said, "I am going to do everything to get you the loan."

So with half a million dollars we bought the building, the land, and all new equipment. Bars, beams, a new foam pit, everything. It was very costly, but very necessary in order to give high-quality instruction.

And as the months go on the kids' progress is so spectacular that the parents are shocked. At the younger levels we are easily winning the state championships, and Dianne Durham is in line to win the national senior championships in the all-around.

Mary Lou, too, is making a great improvement. Though she had the strength and explosiveness when she came to us, she was not too flexible or consistent. But the first time I caught her and spotted her, I could feel that the muscles in her little body were working like springs. "There is something fantastic," I said to myself. "Fantastic." We had begun working on her routines, adding certain skills and making other ones better.

We did not have time to put in a new floor routine, but it was clear to us that we would have to hide some areas and put in evidence her positive ones, to show off her tumbling and let the public participate, to bring out the most from her personality and her expressiveness.

Her vault I thought was a good one for a second vault, a front somersault with a half turn, but we wanted a stronger one. So we began working on twists, and eventually on layouts. On bars she had already created the Retton Salto, where she winds up momentarily on the high bar. We added a half-twisting movement and called it the Retton Salto II. And we worked on her beam, to make it more solid and consistent. By the end of the winter of 1983 we are certain that she is approaching world-caliber. Mary Lou was simply becoming better and better and better.

But I know she's also got to have a name, and 1983 is the last chance before the Olympics. Otherwise there is no way to jump into the Games and make a final sensation. The international gymnastics community has got to know you. That is why so desperately I tried to push Mary Lou that March into the most prestigious competition in the country—the American Cup.

I started first the most normal way by calling up the U.S. Gymnastics Federation, explaining how important it would be for this country to introduce a Mary Lou. A young athlete, a new star with an exciting style and a powerful manner. The idea is to present a surprise, and at the same time to provide the shocking effect what can attract attention of the judges and put the appreciation on the American side.

Well, it was unbelievable. Nobody, but nobody, was even pretending to give a helping hand or provide any kind of support in my try. My several letters to the federation, to the U.S. Olympic Committee, to the several organizations who might be better intended, they were rejected, all of them. "Well," they said, "it is against the rules and policies."

Naturally we never mention to the kids what kind of political games are going on behind the curtains. I never mentioned to Mary Lou what kind of last-moment fight I was doing calling people and trying to beg them and force them to push her in.

Dianne, who had the established reputation, would compete for sure. But I knew that she had injured a hip muscle and might possibly be in some jeopardy.

So finally, without any kind of official approval, I take Mary Lou with us to New York as an alternate. I do not know how, but I tell her one thing: You will compete.

9

MARY LOU
Breaking Through

Bela had tried like a horse to get me into the McDonald's American Cup, but he couldn't. So I knew I'd go to New York as an alternate, but I still figured something might happen. In the meantime I'd sit in the stands and shoot the breeze and watch the competition, see who the Russians brought, the East Germans, and this and that.

I knew Dianne Durham had hurt her hip, but she was still working out, doing her routines, so I thought nothing of it. She'll compete, I figured, because this is a big event.

Anyway, the day before the competition we were working out in another part of Madison Square Garden, and Dianne was going through routines, but not very hard. But Bela was really working me. Gosh, why am I doing five routines, I wondered, and she's competing and doing only one? But I think Bela knew Dianne wasn't going to go. And sure enough, after the workout Bela brought me into the stands and sat down with me.

"I think you're going to compete," he said. "We're pulling Dianne out of the competition."

I just went, "whoooh." It was a shock. But I was completely prepared physically, so it was only a question of getting myself ready mentally to just go out and do it.

When I went out there the next night, it all hit me at once. My first huge international, my first time before a packed house, with all the foreign judges and the eastern European gymnasts, plus the best Americans. There was all this pressure on me because Bela had been telling the federation, "Mary Lou, Mary Lou, she needs this competition, give her a chance."

I can't say I like having pressure on me. I don't think anybody does. But somehow it brings out the best in me. There's always that nervous feeling, that twinge in your stomach, and I don't know if it means I'm anxious or just ready to go. But I think it's something that every competitor has, and I need that.

So even though I felt the pressure, I knew that this was a great opportunity for me. The American Cup has only been around since 1976, but it's become one of the most important gymnastics events in the world. They invite the top twelve men's and women's teams from the last world championships, and all the countries send their best people.

This time the Russians had brought Natalia Yurchenko, who became world champion in the all-around later in the year. The Romanians came with Lavinia Agache, who went on to win world medals in three events. And Julianne McNamara, who'd won the American Cup the two previous years, was competing for us.

With a field like that, there were lots of reasons to be nervous, but the truth was that I had absolutely nothing to lose. I was a last-minute substitute that almost nobody knew and nobody expected anything from. If I did anything at all, I'd be noticed. "This is your chance," Bela told me. "Don't let me down."

When you hear Bela say that, you don't think. You just go.

Each event I hit solid—vault, bars, beam, floor. So I was ahead by five- or six-tenths after the first day. The only problem was, we went clean into the second day; we didn't carry any points over.

But my second day was just as strong. Fortunately, I started off with the vault, which is where I'm always able to jump people and get a lead. Well, I scored a 9.95, which was a meet record, and just went from there. When I'm competing I can tell right off the bat if it'll be a good routine or not. It's just a sense I have. Like on beam, after I do my mount I have a full turn, first thing. I can tell by how I do that if the whole thing's going to be on or not. If I wobble, it's like, "Ohh, no," and I have to slow myself down. But if it's solid, odds are everything will go well from there.

My whole American Cup was like that. Everything came together for me on every apparatus, and the crowd and the competition got me pumped up. I ended up winning the vault and floor, tied Julianne on bars, and beat her by three-tenths of a point for the all-around title.

Even though it was the first time Julianne had lost the American Cup since 1980, she had a higher total score finishing second than she'd had the two years she won it. So Bela, myself, and everybody else knew it was a big breakthrough for me, especially since I did it in New York. Everything always seems bigger when it happens there.

I wound up on the cover of the next issue of *International Gymnast*, which was also a big deal for me. After that I could sense other girls looking at me, watching me warm up, and saying, "She's the one who won American Cup. She beat Yurchenko and Agache and McNamara and everybody."

I'm sure the Russians thought the Americans had been holding me back deliberately, because that's what they do. You go to a major competition and there's this little twelve-year-old you've never seen before who the Russians have decided to spring out. And we come back home and say, "Oh-oh, watch out, they've got another one."

You always see this in the year before the Olympics, because if a country has a new gymnast that they want to bring to the Games, they really have to show her off. That's why Bela wanted to get me into as many events as possible, so the whole spring, summer, and fall of 1983 it seemed I was preparing for a competition.

I'd be in the gym every day, sometimes twice a day, and it became a habit. You put on your leotard and your sweats and do a dance routine at the beginning with the whole team. Then you stretch, do splits, then oversplits, taking between fifteen minutes and half an hour to warm up. Then it's forty-five minutes on each apparatus with only two or three minutes in between, and it's intense. When you have morning workouts you're there by eight, then you go to school, then back to the gym for four hours between five and nine, then homework, then bed.

Coming down to Houston and switching to that kind of a schedule was so different for me. The climate alone took a long time getting used to. "Wait 'til spring and summer," Paige Spiller told me. "It gets *so* hot."

"Aww, it can't be that bad," I said, but it was. With the humidity, it gets so sticky you just pour sweat. You walk into the gym on a muggy day and the bars are so wet they look like somebody washed them. And then with all the pollen, you're always sneezing and stuff.

Everything down there was a change for me. In West Virginia, when I only had two-hour workouts, I could eat dinner at the normal time. Here, I'm eating it at 9:30 at night. The whole functioning of your body is different. I really had to budget my time. So many hours for homework, so many hours for rest. And there really weren't many hours left over. I didn't have time to date. My friends and I would go to a movie occasionally or do some shopping on a Saturday afternoon, but that was about it.

I really had to make sure I stuck to a schedule, because every day I had obligations. If it was Tuesday night and I knew I had a Wednesday morning workout, a little voice would be telling me to go to bed. "Get to sleep," it would say. "You need your eight hours, because you'll be tired if you don't get them. And if you're tired, you won't do good, and you have to do good because you have a competition coming up."

And it was true, because I always did have something coming up. It was either the American Classic or the Caesar's Palace Invitational or American Cup or Championships of the U.S.A. So for a long time that year workouts were very boring, because every day I'd go in and do the same thing. I'd do twenty-five or thirty vaults, then warm up on bars and do five or six bar routines, then warm up on beam, do eight beam routines, then warm up on floor and do two floor routines.

Sometimes they'd change the rotations around, starting on bars instead of vault, but it's really the same thing. It gets a little depressing sometimes, knowing that you're on your fifth bars routine but you still have those eight beams and two floors ahead of you. And it's hard on your body because you don't want to slack off on one event just to save up strength for the others. That's when the proper rest and diet come in handy, because if your body isn't taken care of, you can't perform well. When you're in shape, it's no problem, but it's hard to keep in top shape month after month when one competition follows another.

After a while my body started saying, "Hey, you're getting tired." You can tell because your legs just kind of get heavy, and you feel like when you're running your knees are scraping the floor. I was in shape and doing well, but I just started to get sore. That happens to everybody at some point, usually right after a major competition, when your body has just had enough. You've gone so long and hard that your body just knows it's over and says, oh, stop.

You would think skipping a day here and there wouldn't matter, but it does. You go in after only one missed workout and jump into a split and you're tight. It's weird, but that one day of not stretching or not doing anything means a lot.

Believe me, you really sleep well when you're pushing your body that hard. In May, after about five months of Bela's workouts, a tornado cut the Spillers' house in half, and I slept through it.

It was in the middle of the night and Preston came in to get me. "Get up, get out of bed," he told me.

"Get *out* of here," I groaned, "I'm sleeping." He finally picked me up and carried me out. I walked through the house and suddenly I'm stepping over this tree right in the middle of it and I can't believe it. It's pouring rain, the house is flooded, I was in shock. We spent the rest of the night in a neighbor's house.

The next morning we were in the garage, the only dry place, sitting in lawn chairs looking out at the rain, and I felt this tap on my shoulder.

"Patrick," I said, "*what* do you want?" I turned around and it was my mom and dad. I was freaked out. "What are you doing here?" I said, with my mouth hanging open.

They'd just come down from Fairmont for the weekend, driving all night. "Oh, my God," my mother said, "you're all right." They'd heard on the news that a tornado had hit Houston. "Aww, it won't hit their house," Mom figured. "No way."

It was the only house on the street that was damaged. I mean, it must have been a huge boom, and stupid me sleeps through it. It was great to see my parents, though. I'd always call them once a week, usually on the weekend, and by now I wasn't really homesick any more. It was always worse when I'd had a bad workout. Oohh, I'd think, I want to go home. But when I had a good workout everything was fine, and I was having lots more good workouts than bad ones.

I'd see my parents off and on because they drove down sometimes, but since I came to Karolyi's on New Year's I'd never been home-home. There just wasn't time.

Championships of the U.S.A. were coming up, and after that there'd be pre-Olympics at Los Angeles, trials for the world team, the worlds, the Chunichi Cup in Japan, and then it would be the Olympic year. That's why I finally decided I had to leave school and take correspondence courses instead.

I'd just finished my second semester at Northland Christian, the end of my freshman year. Workouts were getting more demanding, and it had gotten to the point where I couldn't go to school and do gymnastics both. We'd get out of classes at 4 o'clock and I'd have only an hour until gymnastics, and that was really rushing it. By the time I'd finished workouts, had supper, and done my homework, it'd be midnight and time for bed.

It was hard on both my brain and my body. I'd be walking around school thinking about three things at once. "I've got a biology test tomorrow after workout," I'd remember, "but I've also got eight beam routines to do and Martha's going to watch them all." There was so much stress on my mind. I look up to girls who can do both, because it's so difficult. But I'd decided that in my case, where I was definitely shooting for the Olympics, that correspondence courses made more sense.

So I called home. "Dad," I said, "there's no way I can still go to school."

I explained that workouts were really getting demanding, that I was improving, and that the reason I'd gone to Houston in the first place was for gymnastics. Sure, education was important, but at that point gymnastics was my life. The Olympics are a once-in-a-lifetime thing.

It was my decision, but Bela, Martha, and my parents all thought it was a good idea. The correspondence courses in English, math, history, health, and geography would come from the University of Missouri. I'd do them and send them to the board of education back home. That way I could fit my work in when I had the time, still make progress academically, and prepare for the Olympics without a lot of school things to worry about. It might not be the solution for everybody, but at that time, in that situation, it was for me.

Anyway, I was learning plenty of new things in the gymnasium, including at least one thing no woman had ever tried before—a layout Tsukahara vault with a double twist.

Gymnastic tricks are named after the first person who does them in international competition. By the time I came to Bela's I'd already had one named after me—the Retton Salto, also called the Retton Flip—which I'd done on the uneven bars in South Africa the year before. Bars is the hardest to add something new to, since it means changing direction. But because you have so many different ways you can swing and things you can do, bars is one of the best apparatus for creating a new skill.

The Retton was actually an accident. I'd been wanting to do something else; I hadn't planned on landing up on the high bar and just sitting there. But, hey, it was kind of neat. So I tried it a second time and it worked, so Gary Rafaloski, my coach back home in West Virginia, and I started analyzing it and figured out what I had to do.

I'd start by swinging down from a handstand on the high bar, belly-beat the low one, do a front somersault in the pike position, and land seated back on the high bar. Then I'd raise my hands, like it was some sort of magic trick.

I had the Retton pretty well down when I got to Houston, but Bela added a half-twist to it and we had something new. Then in May, with the Championships of the U.S.A. not too far off, we began working on the Tsukahara, or the Sook, for short.

The Sook is named for a man named Mitsuo Tsukahara, who won

a gold medal with the Japanese team at three different Olympics—Mexico City, Munich, and Montreal. It's a layout one-and-a-half back somersault with a full twist, but Bela added a second full twist, which no woman in the world had ever done. Bela likes you to be able to do one trick that no one else does as an eye-catcher for the crowd, because the crowd has a big part in it. If they go crazy for it, it can't help but influence the judges.

"Ohh, we don't know if it is possible," he'd say, "but let's try." Of course, I'd be all pumped up, because I always wanted to do something new, something original. "Anyone else do this?" I'd ask him. "No," he'd say. "Okay. Let's go."

Trying a new trick, or adding something to an old one, can be scary at first. The first time you're lost. "Where am I?" you wonder. "Am I going to land on my head or my feet?" But the next few times you get used to it. There's always the possibility you *will* land on your head or fall in some crazy way, but equipment is so much better these days than it used to be, and the pits are filled with enough foam rubber that it's hard to get hurt. Besides, Bela spots you on everything. He won't let you throw a skill unless he knows you're ready, so I had complete trust in him. When he says do it, you know you can.

So when I first tried the layout Sook with the double twist, it took me a couple of weeks to get it right, to reach the point where I felt comfortable with it. But it was exciting knowing nobody in the world was doing it but me, and that made me want to do the Sook even better.

By the time I was ready to try it in competition I'd done it hundreds of times, and felt fully confident. So Bela decided I'd try it when we went back to Colorado Springs for the American Classic II in the middle of May. We hadn't planned on my doing the Sook there, but I was ahead by a whole bunch when it came time to vault. "Do you want to do it?" Bela asked me. "Sure," I said.

The layout Sook is actually a 10.2 trick, which means that if you do it perfectly you can score even more than a perfect 10, because it's so difficult. Well, I hit the vault just the way I was supposed to, but I didn't stick the landing; I took a little hop. But it still got me a 10, and more important, it was a milestone. I was the first woman in the world to do it.

So a month later I went to Chicago really pumped up for the Championships of the U.S.A. It was my first year as a senior, and everybody, and I mean everybody, was there—Tracee Talavera, who had won it for the last two years; Julianne McNamara; Pam Bileck; Kathy Johnson; Dianne Durham, who was recovered from her hip injury and was back in top form. And everybody else who wanted to be in the Olympics and all the competitions that led up to them.

Well, I did not have a great weekend. I was third behind Dianne and Julianne after the compulsories, and that's where I finished in the all-around, tied with Pam. My marks weren't bad—9.6s on bars and vault, 9.2 on beam and floor—but they weren't what I was hoping for. Dianne won it all by more than a point, and Pam and I finished five-hundredths of a point behind Julianne. And in the event finals, though I finished second on bars and vault, I was fifth on floor, and eighth on beam. So I was a little disappointed and upset with myself. I hate losing, anytime.

My parents tried to help me over it. "You can't be up all the time," they told me. "You'll have bad days, and that was a bad day."

So I went home to Fairmont for the first time since I'd left home, and it was good to sit and think about how much progress I'd made since I'd been in Houston.

I'd learned new skills and improved old ones. I was much more consistent, especially on beam, where Martha had worked me hard. I'd scored my first 10, hadn't lost an all-around from August of 1982 until the 1983 Championships, and had beaten the best women in the country. And because of my beating Yurchenko and Agache and the other top foreigners at the American Cup, my name was beginning to be known overseas, too.

That was the reason why I'd left West Virginia in the first place, to make that breakthrough. I knew I'd have to work harder than I ever had in my life just to make what seemed to be very small technical improvements. I knew I'd be living in a big city halfway across the country, staying with a strange family, going to a new school, and working with a coach I knew about only by rumor. There were times when I'd wondered whether all the sacrifices were worth it. I mean, I probably would have made the Olympic team anyway.

But now that I'd competed against the best gymnasts, I knew how hard you have to work just to move up from the top six to the top two or three, and how tough it is to win big events consistently. So after only six months I could look back at all the good results and really be encouraged.

When I talked things over with my parents, we decided we had made the right decision. We'd timed it out perfectly, having me go down there when I did, and everything was working out so smoothly and so right. If I'd gone to Bela's in 1981, let's say, it would have been much harder knowing I would have to spend three years away from home. This way it was just a temporary thing. At least, that's what we thought.

Before I knew it I was back at Karolyi's, working hard for the next big competitions—the McDonald's Invitational at Los Angeles, which would be the pre-Olympics, and the trials for the U.S. team that would go to the world championships.

By placing third at the Championships of the U.S.A. I would have first choice at most of the major international competitions for the rest of 1983 and the first five months of 1984. The way it works is that you get a ranking based on your placing at Championships, and invitations to events are offered to you according to that. Sometimes the United States gets to send two entries to big meets, sometimes more. Since not every top gymnast is always healthy or available when the chance comes to go somewhere, if you're ranked reasonably high, odds are you'll get to make the trip. Since only Dianne and Julianne were above me on the list, I pretty much had my choice.

Well, at the end of August we went to Los Angeles for the McDonald's International at Pauley Pavilion on the UCLA campus, where the Olympic competition was going to be held in less than a year.

My left wrist was hurting me, but I didn't think too much about it. If you're a gymnast something is always hurting, but you still train. You just have to learn to live with discomfort. That was the way we were brought up, anyway. My mom never babied us if we had a headache or a bellyache. "Well, take an aspirin and go to bed," she'd say. To stay home from school, we really had to be sick. So I grew up with that attitude. If you were active the way I was, you banged things up, and I accepted that. It was part of life.

Once when I was adding a half-twist to the Retton I bruised my ribs so badly that I thought I'd cracked one of them. Every time I'd go short I'd bang them against the low bar, and it killed me. So my dad sent me one of those lightweight flak jackets that quarterbacks wear, and that helped a little.

Everything cracks on me—ankles, knees, wrists. When it's cold and damp outside I just ache all over and I sound like an old wooden railroad trestle. One of my ankles cracks anytime I do anything with it. My mom was a little worried about it, so she took me to have it checked and the doctor said it was no problem. Just one thing rubbing against another and making a sound.

My first instinct whenever anything hurts is, well, it's okay. It's not bad. I'll ice it and it'll be all right in the morning. Or I'll just put some Ben-Gay on it. That comes from working with Bela. He expects you to train with little bruises and aches and pains. You really have to be hurt to lay off.

But this time the wrist was really killing me and I didn't know what was wrong with it. Bela can always read my mind. He can tell from my face and my eyes, and he knew something was really wrong with it. So I went to the team trainer and told him the wrist hurt, and I iced it and took electrical stimulation. Now, I'd had that particular treatment several times before, but this time I was crying it hurt so badly. What a baby, they probably thought, she can't even stand a little stimulation.

I guess you're not supposed to use stimulation on a broken bone, but they didn't know it was broken, and I didn't either. But it was. I hadn't had a big fall or anything, but I guess with all the stress over such a long period of time that bone in the little slot just below my thumb finally cracked.

So I was in a lot of pain all through the competition, but I still wanted to perform. Dianne had a great all-around, with three 9.9s, and won the title, with me second. But I knew that the second day, the event finals, was going to belong to me, so nothing was going to stop me. The wrist was really badly swollen now, but I just taped it as tightly as I could and went out for one of the best days in my career. I won the floor, bars, and vault, accepted my medals, then went back to Houston the next day with a bag of ice on my left hand.

They took me straight to the doctor's, but nothing showed up on the X-ray. Then they took a bone scan and, sure enough, it was broken. So they put the wrist in a cast and told me that it would be eight to twelve weeks. But when you're training with Bela and you have big competitions coming up, you're not going to stay out that long.

I got the cast off in four weeks, but I had missed the trials for the U.S. team that would compete in the 1983 world championships. I still could have been ready to perform, and with my showing at Championships and what I'd done all year I probably could have petitioned for a place on the team. But there was a team rule that you had to have been at the training camp in West Germany, which was a month long. That kept me off the team and out of the worlds.

For one reason or another a lot of the girls—me, Dianne, Tracee, Marie Roethlisberger—didn't compete in Budapest. The team finished seventh, and no American girl won a medal. Our best finish in the all-around was eleventh by Kathy Johnson, and the best placing in an event final was a sixth by Julianne in the vault.

As expected, the eastern Europeans won everything in sight. The Russians took the team title over Romania and East Germany, and Natalia Yurchenko won the all-around with a pair of 10s in vault and floor. And two of Bela's former girls, Ecaterina Szabo and Lavinia Agache, won seven medals between them in the individual events.

"Didn't that hurt you, to be missing from a big international meet like that?" people asked me. I didn't think so. I'd already beaten Yurchenko and Agache, and Boriana Stoyanova of Bulgaria, who'd won the gold in vault and the bronze on floor. It would have been nice to have gone to a world championship, since I'd never had the chance, but there was still the Chunichi Cup in Japan coming up in December.

A lot of the world's top gymnasts would be there, too, and it would be that much closer to the Olympic Games. It would also be a chance for me to prove to international judges that the American Cup hadn't been a fluke.

I'd won it, but it had been in my own country and I'd caught people a little by surprise. No American had ever won the Chunichi Cup, and it wasn't hard to see why. It's early in the season, it's overseas before a strange audience, the field is top-notch, and the judging politics are tough. Whew, is it a rough meet.

I knew that Bela was wondering how I'd deal with a major competition in a foreign country, and I wanted to find out, too. Traveling overseas was nothing new for me, and I'd been to Japan when I was a junior. But Chunichi Cup is completely different.

There are three big events every year that everybody focuses in on and goes all out for—the world championships, American Cup, and Chunichi Cup. But here in the States nobody knows about Chunichi Cup. Because it's on the other side of the world, American television doesn't cover it live, and there's not much about it in the newspapers. But the important gymnastics countries send their best people to it, and they're all in top shape.

Well, in 1983 the East Germans sent Maxi Gnauck, who was world champion on bars. The Bulgarians sent Stoyanova, the world champion in vault. The Russians sent Yelena Shushunova, who they thought was going to be better than Yurchenko. And Dianne Durham and I represented the United States.

Since I hadn't been at Budapest, Chunichi Cup was my world championships, and I wanted to be well prepared for it. So we went over to Nagoya a few days early, because it takes some time to recover from jet lag, get your system back to normal, and adjust to the differences in daily life.

When you're a gymnast, you get used to doing things a certain way all the time. You're training in your hometown, you're used to the food, the weather, the gym, and a set workout on equipment you're familiar with. But when you go overseas, everything from the language to the diet to the uneven bars is just different enough to throw you off. In a sport like ours, where concentration is so important and the margin between winning and placing fourth is often a couple of tenths of a point, those little things can become pretty big.

So it was important for me to go over there completely ready, both physically and mentally. At the same time, I wanted to treat Chunichi Cup like any other competition. If you dwell too much on how important it is, it works against you. The best way to approach any big meet is that it's a chance to show how hard you've worked and how well you can perform your routines. If you're well prepared and you run through the skills the way you know you can, the scores will show that.

When I got to Nagoya, I felt really confident on every apparatus. The way the event was structured, Dianne and I each competed in two event finals on the first night. I wound up beating Angelika Schennikova, one of the Russians, and a Chinese girl named Wu Wenli, to win the vault, and I was fourth on floor, but just fifteen-hundredths of a point behind Gnauck and Shushunova, who tied for first place.

And the second night in the all-around I beat Shushunova, Dianne, and Gnauck, and won it all. I just really felt comfortable from the first rotation, and everything came together for me. The crowd was very fair, and I was hitting everything solid.

Well, that made an even greater impression than my winning the American Cup. I was outside of my country, I'd beaten a greater variety of gymnasts, and it was only eight months before the Olympics. So even though it didn't get a lot of publicity back in America, I could see people taking more notice of me after that, especially in other countries.

At the beginning of 1984 I saw an article where they were talking with a bunch of Eastern Bloc girls. "Who is your biggest threat for the 1984 Games?" the question was. "Mary Lou Retton," was the answer. Well, that was weird for me, knowing that my name was probably bigger in Europe than it was right here in the United States. It opened my eyes to the fact that they were threatened by me over there, and that made me feel great.

Those other countries aren't stupid. The coaches all know, and they knew I was with Bela and knew I'd keep getting better and stronger. So I'm sure they went back after Chunichi Cup and said, "You've gotta watch out for this little American."

But for a long time I'd been frustrated in this country because I couldn't seem to get over that hump of Tracee Talavera and Julianne McNamara in people's minds. For most of 1983 I'd gone up against them and beaten one or both of them, but the next time I'd go to a competition the advertisements would still say, "Featuring Tracee Talavera and Julianne McNamara." I wanted *my* name to be up there, too, but it takes a while and there's nothing you can do about it.

"I deserve it," I'd tell myself, "I did good." But I also realized that both Tracee and Julianne had been in the sport a lot longer than I had been, and people were used to seeing them and hearing about them. Tracee had been on the U.S. team since 1979. She'd won the 1980 Olympic trials, and had been national all-around champion twice. Julianne had been on the Olympic team, too, had won a medal on bars at the 1981 Worlds in Moscow, and had placed higher (seventh) in the all-around than any American woman in history. And Dianne was the 1983 U.S. champion.

I hadn't done any of that. If I kept winning, I realized, people would know me and my name would be recognized, too.

I think it helped me, not being considered number one at that time. Because if you start thinking, hey, I'm number one, people kill you. That's what they do. They want you up there, but then they're after you.

The important thing was that I had proven I belonged at the world-class level and that there wasn't anybody I couldn't beat. Everything I'd hoped to accomplish in one year at Bela's I'd done. If I wanted to see how far I'd come, all I had to do was watch one of Bela's newer gymnasts. I used to do it like that, I'd think. I used to work out like that. And I thought it was good.

Now I'd noticed the difference. And by the beginning of 1984 I'd noticed something else. For a year I'd seen the words "Mary Lou Retton" and "Olympic hopeful" in magazines. Now I was seeing them together.

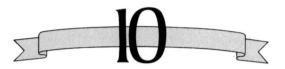

MARY LOU
Sweat, Pain, and Other Things

When I returned to Karolyi's after winning Chunichi Cup, we got back to work right away. All the big competitions—Caesar's Palace Invitational, American Cup, Championships of the U.S.A.—were coming up, and we had new Olympic-year routines to learn and other skills to sharpen. And I was looking forward to going head-to-head with Dianne Durham every day. Ever since I'd come to Houston a year earlier we had been determined to outdo each other. She wanted to beat me, and I wanted to beat her, and I'm sure that helped us both.

I don't think it was an accident that she became national champion and that I won in Japan. When every workout is like the Olympic trials, you both can't help but improve. We'd gone everywhere together in 1983—Las Vegas, Colorado Springs, Chicago, New York, Los Angeles, Nagoya. Sometimes she'd beat me, sometimes I'd beat her, but it was usually close.

We had different personalities. Dianne opened up in her own sort of way, but she wasn't really the easygoing type. Me, I was always talking and laughing and joking around. Dianne and I still had a lot in common, though. Our body types, the events we were best in, our drive, and the one thing we were at Karolyi's for—to make the Olympic team.

And then one day in February she was gone. Everybody realized it right away because it's unusual when somebody doesn't show up for workout. Gosh, you think, she must be in the hospital. Because at Bela's you come if you're sick, sore, whatever.

"Where's Dianne?" I asked Bela. He growled and grunted something.

"What?" I said. And he told the whole group of us that she'd left the gym and gone up to Fort Worth to train with Scott Crouse. She'd left him a short note. We were shocked. Was this a joke? But it wasn't.

Well, I thought, there goes my competition. Because that's exactly how it was. Beth Pope, who'd been one of Bela's best gymnasts, wasn't around anymore. And Kerry Haynie, who was going to qualify for the Olympic trials, wasn't at my same level.

"You're just going to have to keep going on," Bela told me. "Dianne's not going to be here, and you're not going to be pushing each other. You'll just have to push yourself."

So I was resigned to pretty much having to go it alone. But after a week or so the telephone rang at the Spillers' house. It was Bela.

"Are you sitting down?" he asked.

"No."

"Sit down."

"What?" I said. "Tell me. What's wrong?"

"Guess who is coming to our gym?"

"Who?"

"Julianne McNamara."

Well, that was the last person in my mind. Julianne coming here? She'd originally been training in Oregon with Tracee Talavera. Then she'd gone to southern California to work with SCATS and Don Peters. Now she was coming here.

Dianne had gone to Forth Worth. Kathy Johnson had changed clubs, too, going to SCATS. And the summer before Tracee had left Oregon to train in the Bay Area. What are those girls doing? I wondered.

Because those are major moves to make. The adjustments to a new city, a new gym, new coaching, and this and that. Maybe there's a little desperation there. The Olympics are coming up in six months and your training isn't going the way you want it to. Maybe you think, If I'm going to make a move, I'm going to make it now. When I asked Julianne about it, she just said that she'd needed to make a change, and we didn't discuss it much further.

I'd competed against her a lot in 1983, and we'd talked, but we weren't close friends. Our makeups were so different. She was the complete opposite of me. That's why I was curious to see how Julianne would adjust to the atmosphere at Karolyi's, to the workouts, and to Bela. Just wait, I'd think, watching one of Julianne's routines. Just wait 'til he sees *that*. Of course, I'm sure Dianne had thought the same thing when I first came down there, too.

So it was probably hard for Julianne at first because she'd been at the top for a long time and thought that what she was doing was really good. But after a couple of weeks with us I think she was wondering whether she'd really made a big mistake. She wasn't used to the atmosphere, she wasn't used to the workouts, and she wasn't used to someone picking every routine apart and having her do them over and over.

I think Bela could sense Julianne had a quiet personality, though, so he never really yelled at her. Me, he didn't care. "You have lost your mind," he'd say. "You are crazy. Your head is full of rocks. You should not be doing gymnastics. You should be planting flowers." But you have to communicate with each person differently, and I guess the low-key approach was the way to deal with Julianne.

It was great to have somebody at her level to compete against again, but our rivalry was different. There wasn't the head-to-head fighting that Dianne and I used to do. Part of it was the difference in our personalities, but a lot of it was that we were strong in different events. Julianne was national champion on bars, and she'd won a medal at the 1981 world championships. She was more lean and leggy than I was, and she looked great up there.

So when I was chalking up in workout and getting ready to go on, I'd watch her and notice how well she extended, and I learned a lot that way. And she learned from me on other events, like vault and floor. It worked out well for both of us, having her there.

At the same time, workouts were becoming more enjoyable. Because the Olympics were only a few months away, we were working on new routines and learning new skills, so it was fun. You'd almost look forward to it.

During 1983 there were so many competitions following each other that you'd just work on the same routines for weeks at a time, and it got very boring. Now, though, there was always new stuff to work on. On beam, for example, Martha and I were working on some different tricks, because I'd really made a big improvement there and I was feeling good about competing on beam.

I think for a while the judges had thought, Oh, she was lucky. She stayed on today. So I wanted to show people that, hey, I'm not the same old girl who jumped down all the time. It amazed me what I could do up there now. Just from Martha stretching them every day, my legs had gotten to where they were flat against the beam and couldn't go any more. I never in my life dreamed I could do that.

But the biggest change was in my floor exercise. The one I'd had was good, fast, dynamic with lots of poses, done to orchestrated classical music. Yet there's a point when you need a change, and with the McDonald's American Cup coming up again, Bela thought it was time.

So he got Geza Pozsar, who'd been his choreographer with the Romanian team, to make up a new routine for me with different music—"Johnny, My Friend." It was a kind of gypsy-type thing, and Emilia Eberle had used it when she won the 1979 world title on floor.

"It fits you like a glove," Bela kept saying, and it did. It was *me*. "I love it," I said, the first time they played me the music. "Let's do it."

It took two or three days for me to get the whole routine together and get little parts comfortable, but all of us knew it would be great. So we put it in a week before the American Cup, and I went back to New York to defend my title.

The Russians and East Germans had pulled out at the last minute, saying that they were worried about security for their athletes in the United States. But there were still plenty of other world-class gymnasts there, because this was the last major international competition before the Olympics, and whoever won it would build up momentum that she could carry into the Games.

So the Romanians sent Laura Cutina, who went on to finish fifth in the Olympic all-around. Hana Ricna of Czechoslovakia, who had won the silver medal on beam at the world championships, was there, too. So was Zhou Qiurui, who was a member of China's bronze-medal team at Los Angeles, and Elke Heine from West Germany, who made the Olympic all-around final. And, of course, Julianne, who'd won American Cup twice.

Well, when I got a 10 on my floor routine the first day, it seemed like a good omen for me. The second day, the one that counts, just went really well on every apparatus. I scored 9.95 on bars, 9.80 on beam, and 9.75 on floor. And I got another 10, this time on vault. So I wound up winning the title again, ahead of Cutina and Julianne, and it gave me another nice boost as far as confidence was concerned.

Just having that one year's experience made such a big difference for me. After six or seven competitions I'd learned how to handle big crowds watching me. It's a matter of blocking them out when they would be a distraction, and bringing them in when you need them.

On beam, when ten million photographers are shooting or ABC comes right up in your face just before you go on, you want to screen it all out because you have to keep your concentration. But when you're on floor, you want them all involved. After a while you learn how to deal with it.

By now it wasn't a problem for me. I'd done well in all kinds of competitions in all sorts of circumstances, and since my wrist had healed, I'd just kept winning. From the fall of 1983 through the Olympic Games I won fourteen all-around titles in a row. After a while you sort of get into a winning rhythm, where you are doing well in workouts every day so you bring a lot of confidence into your competitions. When you win them you feel that your hard work has been justified, which makes you want to improve even more in workout. And that's what helps you keep winning.

So as the months went by in 1984 I was feeling more solid and confident all the time, and as the Championships of the U.S.A. got closer our workouts became more intense. We'd go to the gym in the morning, doing compulsory routines over and over and over, trying to make them more spectacular. Then in the evenings we'd come back and go full out with the optionals.

Compulsories get really monotonous because you have to perform everything by the book and there's only so much you can do. But optionals are fun because you can do your own thing, have your own style. Still, you have to learn how to execute both perfectly, so we were just spending hours and hours at Karolyi's every day. That's why a few months before the Games I decided to stop all my correspondence courses and just focus on my training.

"I'm concentrating on workouts," I told myself, "and that's it." So I'd go to the gym in the morning, return home and sleep, then go back to the gym. That was my life. "Don't go home and go shopping," Bela would tell us, because he wanted us resting.

So I'd take a hot bath and read a book or watch "The Guiding Light," because that puts you in another world and gets your mind off gymnastics. Still, after doing routines hundreds and hundreds of times, they become part of you.

Sometimes I'd find myself going through workouts in my sleep. I'd be doing something on bars and I'd just keep going around and around and around and it wouldn't end. I'd have to sit up and finish the thing so I could stop. Other times I'd have dreams where I'd just keep seeing myself doing it wrong and crashing and hurting. Or maybe I'd see myself doing it perfectly. Before major competitions the dreams would be more positive, because Bela would have been putting it in our minds to go for it, hard, and not hold back.

Ideally, you *should* be able to do the routines in your sleep. Someone should be able to pull you out of bed and put you on an apparatus and have you do the whole thing in your pajamas without a mistake. That's what Bela has in mind, to have you repeat things in workout so often that they become second nature.

There were times when I didn't think it was fair, us having to work that hard just to go to the same competitions everybody else was going to. Gee, here we are working so hard and placing first and second,

I'd think, and girls from other teams who're doing nothing like we are in workouts are still getting third and fourth.

Finally, though, I began to understand. Working hard becomes a habit, a serious kind of fun. You get your self-satisfaction from pushing yourself to the limit in workouts, knowing that all the effort, sweat, and pain is going to pay off for you. There is no easy way, and when we'd be at events with girls from other clubs you could notice the difference in intensity. You didn't see it in their faces. It just wasn't there.

So when springtime came we were still working hard as ever, always with the Olympics in mind. Then one day in April someone told me that the Russians were boycotting.

My phone was ringing nonstop that whole day with reporters asking for my reaction. At first I was really angry about it. Oh, God, I thought, here they go again. They're not going to start this stuff. I know how disappointed Julianne and Tracee and Kathy Johnson had been in 1980 when the American team couldn't go to Moscow. And I began thinking about Natalia Yurchenko and Olga Mostepanova and the rest of the Russian girls not being able to compete this time, and I felt sorry for them.

I'd never gotten to know the Russians. I mean, at the American Cup and Chunichi Cup, I'd be smiling and they didn't even smile back. You just couldn't communicate with them. Maybe they're told to be like that, I decided. Still, even though I was upset about their not coming to Los Angeles, I sympathized with them. They'd been working hard, too, and had the same dream I did. To have that big letdown must have hurt.

I wanted to go up against them, and it disappointed me that it wouldn't be happening. "But, you know, the Olympics are always going to be the Olympics," I told myself. "People aren't going to say, 'Well, she won the gold but the Russians weren't there.'" As far as I was concerned, nothing had changed for me. I still had workouts, I still had the Championships of the U.S.A. and the Olympic trials coming up. So I just set my mind on preparing for them.

The Championships of the U.S.A. are important in any year, but in an Olympic year they also have a lot to do with who makes the team. To qualify for trials you have to finish in the top twenty, and 40 percent of your score carries over. If you don't do well at Championships, you're at a real disadvantage when you go to trials. So there's a lot of pressure there. I wasn't worried about qualifying for trials, and I was pretty sure I'd make the team. I mean, I'd been number one all year and my training had been going well, so I was confident.

I probably could have played it safe at Championships, especially since I'd torn this plantar fascia in one of my feet and it was hurting me to walk. But I really wanted to win, for a couple of reasons. Being champion of your country means something, and I hadn't done that yet. And I wanted that formal number-one ranking, just to have the freedom to go anywhere for competitions. That meant a lot to me.

Since I was ranked third, based on what I'd done at the 1983 Championships, I wasn't an automatic choice for any big event where the United States could only enter two gymnasts. For me to go, either Julianne or Dianne had to be unavailable. So in a way the 1984 Championships was the most important event of the year for me, but I tried to approach it as just another meet. All I had to do was perform my routines the same way I did in workouts, and I figured I'd be all right.

My foot I didn't worry about. I had a cortisone shot, taped it tight, and went out there. Besides, during competitions you don't feel injuries.

My compulsories, where I got a 9.9 on vault, I thought were solid. And I was really pleased with my optionals—a 10 on vault, 9.85 on floor, 9.8 on bars. Only my beam, 9.4, was off. So I beat Julianne for the all-around title, won the event finals in floor and vault, and tied for third on beam.

The surprise was Dianne, who finished seventh after winning the title the year before. You could tell that some of her skills had gotten rusty since leaving Bela's. Dianne didn't have the same flexibility anymore, and she'd picked up some bad habits. She just wasn't the same gymnast she'd been in Houston.

Well, a couple of days later Dianne was back at Karolyi's, and it was like she'd never been away. She just got right back into the routine, which was really intense because we only had three weeks until trials and there were four of us who'd qualified—myself, Julianne, Dianne, and Kerry Haynie.

We were all really pushing and psyched for it, and that was neat. It was "Karolyi's Going to Trials." And for me it went from one extreme to the other as far as publicity was concerned. Before we used to call people for interviews; it was like, you know, this girl is going someplace. Now we almost had to turn people down. I found doing interviews pretty easy, actually. You just tell 'em what you think. I enjoy talking about myself and my sport, and I really like meeting new people anyway. So speaking to sportswriters or going on television is pretty natural for me, and it was fun to be recognized for something you'd accomplished.

As trials got closer, I found myself really looking forward to them. That's when people start getting excited about the Olympics. ABC covers everything live, and you can sense that atmosphere that only comes around every four years.

It was an even bigger thing this time, because the Olympics were in our country for the first time in fifty-two years, and because the Americans hadn't competed in 1980. So there had been eight years to build up to it, and there was the feeling that this was the strongest women's gymnastics team the U.S.A. had ever had.

People said that the trials would be more pressure than the Olympics, but it wasn't all that true in my case. After Championships I was in first place going in, so there wasn't quite the burden on me that there was on other girls. The top four finishers were guaranteed places on the team, and I was pretty sure I'd be among them. So I didn't think I had that much to worry about, not as long as I competed up to my abilities.

My foot was still hurting when I got to Jacksonville, so my plan was to go in and hit solid, just go by the book. There was no reason to try anything risky. My marks in compulsories were good enough to keep me in first place, two-tenths of a point ahead of Julianne. And I knew I'd do well in optionals, because Bela had worked us so hard there.

The big pressure was on Dianne, Kathy Johnson, and Tracee

Talavera. Dianne had been seventh at Championships, and Tracee eighth, and you had to be eighth to even have a chance of making the team. And Kathy, who'd been sixth at Championships, had problems with a handstand in compulsories at trials, got a 7.65 on bars, and dropped to ninth.

Well, after the floor exercise in optionals, Dianne had moved up to sixth and a good vault would have brought her up even more. But somehow she landed short and sprained her ankle, and that's how it ended for her.

I remember seeing her sitting in a chair, crying, with Bela standing next to her. She had to pull out and use her scores from the Championships for bars and beam. That dropped her to ninth place, behind Kathy. After all that work, after winning the national championship just one year earlier, Dianne missed a chance at the Olympics by two-tenths of a point. I felt so sorry for her.

I was more fortunate. My foot held up well enough, and I had good, consistent optionals—9.85 on vault and floor, 9.75 on bars, and 9.60 on beam. So when it was over and they'd figured out all the mathematics, which were complicated, I'd finished in first place ahead of Julianne, Michelle Dusserre, and Pam Bileck.

All of us were assured of competing in the Olympics. But the next four girls—Lucy Wener, Tracee, Marie Roethlisberger, and Kathy—had to go to a special training camp and only two of them would make the team from there. So the pressure was off myself and Julianne, and for the next couple of weeks we just concentrated on sharpening and polishing our routines, and doing some summer camps with Bela.

My right knee had been bothering me through Championships and trials, yet I didn't think anything of it. It was hurting on landings, but so what? You work with the aches and pains. So we were in Louisville for a camp in the middle of June, and on a Wednesday, when we were doing an exhibition, Julianne and I were warming up, tumbling, and the knee was hurting rather a lot. It was clicking and I felt something moving, but I didn't want to say anything because the Olympics were only six weeks away. Just keep it to yourself, I thought, and it'll be okay.

We finished the exhibition and sat down to sign autographs, but when I went to stand up, I couldn't. The knee had locked on me. Oh, my God, I thought. Bela's reaction was what it always is when he's a little bit scared. He gets mad. "I don't know what you're doing," he growled.

"It'll be okay, it'll be okay," I told him. "I'll just ice it tonight." That's always my reaction whenever anything hurts. But when I got back to my room, the knee was huge. So I put a big thing of ice on it and went to sleep. Please, *please*, I thought, let it be all right in the morning.

But it wasn't. When I woke up the whole bed was wet from melted ice, and the knee was still swollen. I couldn't walk on it. By now Bela was a little more scared but he wouldn't let me know it. "Oh, it will be okay," he kept saying, but I don't think he believed it.

I was lying in this little office thing in the gym, just in shock. "I can't believe this just happened," I was moaning. "Why me?"

I was absolutely miserable, and Julianne was sitting there with her eyes all wide. "Oh, it'll be okay," she told me.

"It'll be okay?" I said. "Here I can't move my knee, and the Olympics are next month? Right."

I was crying now, and they took me to the Humana Hospital to have the knee checked. "You're going to have to have surgery," they told me, and I was horrified.

"No, you don't understand," I said. "I have the Olympics coming up. I'm on the team, I'm supposed to compete. Isn't there anything you can do? I don't believe this. The Olympics are only a month away."

Well, they brought me back to the gym and told Bela, and I was still crying, all upset. It's over, I thought. Over. I was first in the trials, and here I can't even perform in the Games.

Bela was trying to comfort me. "We can do it," he said. "We can do it. We still have six weeks."

Doctor David Rollo, who had invited Bela to teach at the camp, arranged for the hospital's private jet to take me right away to Richmond to see Doctor Richard Caspari, who's considered one of the best knee surgeons in the world. He told me that some cartilage had broken off into a couple of pieces, and that one of them had gotten caught in the

123

knee joint and made it lock. That's why I couldn't straighten it out or walk on it.

So Doctor Caspari said he'd have to poke into it at the Humana hospital and do arthroscopy, which is where you make small incisions and go into the joint with tiny instruments. That way you only have these little dots instead of this huge shark bite, and you can make a quicker recovery. Still, it was my first surgery, and I was scared to death. "They're going to give me that little cap and gown to wear," I thought, "and they'll put me to sleep."

My parents had driven all night from Fairmont because I'd called them from Louisville, and they were there to give me some comfort and support. They didn't know how bad it was, and Bela and I really didn't, either. But the doctor did clean surgery. He didn't go in and hit anything that would have made the knee more sore or swollen or whatever.

Afterwards Dr. Caspari came in to tell me how it had gone. "You can do it," he said. "The surgery went clean. You can do it." And that gave me the go-ahead to fight, to just go.

"It can be done if you're really determined," the medical people said, "and if you really *want* to do it." I don't know if they were just telling me that for my confidence to make me feel good, or not. Bela was a little shaky on the subject. I don't know if he was sure we had enough time. But I *had* to do it, and I wanted to. So that same night I was back on the jet, headed for Houston.

I slept most of the next day, but the day after that I was back in the gym, bending the knee. Ohh, it was so sore. But I was determined. I *had* to do this. I knew I was lucky that it happened when it did, because if the knee had locked just one week later, I wouldn't have made it. I know I wouldn't have. Because I did about three months' rehabilitation in two weeks.

"Take your time," Doctor Caspari had said, but I couldn't.

"You don't understand," I'd told him. "I have Olympics in a month. I have to get back in shape."

Just getting the bends out of the knee was tough. I would bend it, straighten it, bend it again. But except for the stiffness, I had no real pain. I was still scared for those first few days, wondering what was going to happen. The doctor had given me one of those braces, but I wasn't wearing it because I think it makes you relax. You don't use your knee as much and the muscles get weaker. So I was icing the knee before and after workout, and Bela was real positive because things were going so good and I was having no pain with it. He couldn't believe it, and I couldn't either.

"Don't hurt yourself," Martha was saying. "Don't go so hard." But the knee was holding up well and there was so much work to do.

There were certain things I couldn't do, like tumbling and landings from bars and beam. Yet there were still ways to get in a good, full workout without risking any injury. I could still do bars for the most part. The knee hurt a little when it was loose there, hanging in the air, but I could manage the upper-body stuff. I could still do handstands on beam, which was important for my confidence because I at least could keep in touch with it.

Bela developed a good exercise for when I was doing bicycle. He'd put my floor music on and I would pedal regularly, doing the dance movements, with my arms. But when the tumbling part came, I'd sprint as fast as I could on the bike, simulating it, and it really made me tired. At first I was laughing. "Oh, I can do this," I said. But after twenty minutes I was just dying. Bela would put the tape on several times, and that helped build up my endurance. So I was able to stay in pretty good shape and still do parts of routines.

And in less than two weeks, after lots of bicycling, swimming, leg weights, and bending, I was able to do tumbling, landing, everything. I knew that eventually I'd have to have full surgery on the knee, sometime when I had the time to be on crutches. But I didn't have time then.

By the beginning of July Julianne and I were going twice a day, compulsories in the morning, optionals at night. Our morning workouts got longer; we were in there for two, two-and-a-half hours, instead of ninety minutes, and we'd go longer in the evening, too. They were great workouts, really solid. It would be routine, routine, routine, get off the event.

Bela still had his comments—stretch here, point there—but we felt comfortable. It was just a matter of polishing everything. By now we'd done those routines hundreds of times.

I had a new beam routine that I could do in my sleep. I'd improved the Retton Flip on bars. I had a floor exercise that fit me like a glove. And a vault that no other woman in the world could do. I was a different gymnast than the fourteen-year-old who'd shown up in Houston eighteen months earlier. Just watching myself on tape, I could see that.

My body was leaner and much more flexible, and I had control of it. It wasn't flying wild all over the place anymore, with Bela shaking his head no-no-no.

That was the difference. If I'd stayed in West Virginia I might still have made the Olympic team, and possibly have had a chance for a medal in one of the event finals. And people would have said, well, she did pretty well—for her. And I would have always thought, what if. . . .

Now there were no ifs. I was going to Los Angeles—and going for the gold.

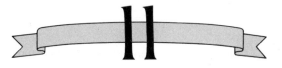

BELA

This Beautiful Dream

When Mary Lou wins the American Cup in 1983 everything changes overnight. The media, they figure out immediately that something is boiling in Bela's kitchen. Hey, they think, better we pay attention.

So with increasing propaganda around her Mary Lou started to become known around the country as one of the coming-up stars. She achieved a phenomenal, fantastic series of victories, going from competition to competition, winning, winning, winning. She and Dianne literally swept away everybody at the pre-Olympic event at Los Angeles that summer, but they both got injured. Mary Lou hurt her wrist, and Dianne her knee. So we decided neither of them should go to the world championships in Budapest, for a couple of reasons.

To send them over there semi-injured and push them into the mouth of the lion of all those Socialist countries was not a good idea. I was not a member of the American coaching staff, and without me there to support them, to make connections, to fight if necessary, they could not win. So I did not want to compromise them, to see them finishing under seventh place and end forever their chance to be Olympic champion. "I don't want you guys to go," I told them. "Is no reason to go."

I knew what would happen in Budapest. The Russians and Romanians would win everything, and the United States would have a near-disaster. Was no question. Well, that is exactly what happened. "You guys should be happy," I told Mary Lou and Dianne, "that you weren't over there."

Still, it was important to show that they were definite Olympic contenders, so I was happy that both girls could go to the Chunichi Cup in Japan in December. I knew it would be the last chance to line up against the best Russians, the best Bulgarians, the best East Germans, the cream of the world. I also wanted to see how they would act outside the American borders, where the circumstances and the pressures are different. So when Mary Lou won the competition with Dianne coming third, we had accomplished what we set out to do.

The Russians were getting crazy because they knew my gymnasts had beaten them so many times in my life. "Bela, you are killing us again," they told me. "What the hell has happened?"

So I was looking forward to having Mary Lou and Dianne continue their aggressive rivalry at the gym, having their own personal Olympic trials every day in workout. But then Dianne, without any kind of previous notice, left the club. Her mother left a short note at the office, letting us know Dianne was unhappy, that she felt she was not getting the attention, and that's how we figured out what happened. It was her decision, but I think Dianne was getting bad advice from gymnastic-related people. But obviously we continue, and put even more accent on Mary Lou's preparation.

And in a week or so comes Julianne McNamara to train with us. She had been on the 1980 Olympic team and was still a top gymnast, but she was frustrated and disappointed. Her performances were going down more and more, and she had gotten to the point where there was no more reasons for her even to do gymnastics. The last big slap in her face had been the 1983 world championships, where people had said she'd do great, but Julianne wound up sixteenth in the all-around.

By now she was mentally shaken, and physically out of shape. She had started to hate the sport, and was working less and less. By the time she got here from SCATS, her previous club, you felt she will never make it.

So it was a question of building Julianne back up, both physically and psychologically, and we didn't have much time, only a couple of weeks. It was not an easy thing for her, and because she was so out of shape and so down I probably gave Julianne more adjustment time than anybody else who came to us.

Having Mary Lou in the same gym was good for her, just as it had been for Mary Lou to have Dianne there. But it was not the same. Because their strengths were different, the same life-or-death rivalry was not there. Mary Lou knew that Julianne would be better on the bars. I don't care, she thought. She will never vault like me. She will never tumble like me. So Julianne and Mary Lou were not what Dianne and Mary Lou had been, like tigers watching each other. But when we went to Championships of the U.S.A., they were clearly the top two girls there.

Mary Lou won easily, with Julianne right behind. But Dianne, who only one year before had been champion of the country, finished seventh. She came there out of shape, technically sloppy, and without her well-known fighting spirit.

Well, after the championships suddenly Dianne came back. Normally we never close to anybody the door, but we have only two weeks until Olympic trials. This short time wasn't enough to prepare her and get her back in the shape she had been losing for four months. But we try. And by the time we go to Jacksonville for the trials we had already some solid workouts. The atmosphere was good. The fighting spirit was back, even though not as intense. Mary Lou was way ahead, with Julianne solidly behind her. Dianne was third, trying desperately to get back.

Dianne did well in compulsories, but after the optional vault she sprained her ankle and decided she cannot continue. So she misses the Olympic team by the smallest margin, tenths of a point. I thought back to how it had been with Nadia and Teodora Ungureanu, and how it happens that Nadia is the one to get the whole recognition.

Ungureanu was still one of the best gymnasts in the world, but she never got the fame and the great glory. The same thing happened here. Mary Lou and Dianne were two great athletes, very close in

129

all ways. One got the opportunity to become Olympic champion. The other lost maybe forever her chance.

There were some similarities between Nadia and Mary Lou—that strong, aggressive style, not giving up, making fantastic performances when everybody else is shaking. That goal-oriented, total dedication. But the difference is that Nadia had eight years to prepare for the Olympic Games. Mary Lou had just one and a half. So it was a great professional satisfaction for me, helping to build a talented but inconsistent young girl into a solid and powerful athlete.

What we did here was a compression of everything. It was like a concentrated soup in a small bowl, but excellently tasty. We were always in a time crisis, running like a marathoner against the clock. Just give us one more week, one more day, I would think. Because we were really using every minute.

But Mary Lou was a fighter. Her natural optimism and positiveness turn these hard workouts into exciting, spectacular shows. She is all the time performing unique, difficult skills, taking the challenge and the risk with a smile and joy in her face. Her progress was incredible.

Her impressive series of victories, being the only undefeated gymnast in the world from the fall of 1983 through the Olympic Games, made Mary Lou be considered by the international gymnastics community as one of the strongest Olympic contenders. Then, when everything was going just right, when I started to believe nothing can stop her from the Olympic victory, suddenly, unexpectedly, when we had just a few more weeks to go, comes the disaster, that day in Louisville.

During regular tumbling practice—nothing difficult, nothing extraordinary—Mary Lou mentioned that something was sore in her knee. The next morning when she woke up it was all blocked and swollen. Can you imagine? All the efforts, could they be ruined now? "God," I said, "if there is any justice in the world, it will not happen. It cannot be ruined, this beautiful dream, when we get so close to it." How many days do we have? That was the first thing in my mind. Immediately I counted the days, the hours, the minutes. "Every second," I say to myself, "is very important."

So we take Mary Lou in a private airplane to Richmond, where

Doctor Caspari performed arthroscopic surgery. He was pretty optimistic about her knee recovering, but to compete in less than six weeks was almost excluded. I didn't push the issue because when you are asking questions doctors are most of the time conservative, very cautious. They don't jump too far away, they never encourage you to start something earlier because that is their nature.

Well, Doctor Caspari told me that the area basically was repaired but he could not guarantee that no other little cartilage pieces would come out. But right now, he said, is okay. He indicated a fifteen-day recovery program, and said for her to gradually, slowly start to walk.

But we could not afford to wait that long, so the day after we get back Mary Lou returned to the gym and we began the nightmare of rehabilitation. She was trying to walk with tears in her eyes, but Mary Lou showed a tremendous will to recover. Very few athletes in similar situations, knowing the short time frame, would even try to get back into shape.

Well, our doctor in Houston, Doctor Hermon, devised for her a special rehabilitation program. We added to it jogging, swimming, and the ergonometric bicycle so we could keep up the rhythm and endurance without performing hard tumbling skills. So after ten days Mary Lou's physical potential was almost at the same level as before. After thirteen days she began to tumble again. At the same time the federation people wanted a written indication of whether she would line up for the Olympic Games.

I knew there were some people who would prefer that she not show up, who were looking for a reason to keep Mary Lou off the team. You will never experience that satisfaction, I thought, to have her written accordance that she will not show up. Mary Lou will be there, even on one leg.

The whole thing was a political ballgame, and it made for a complicated situation. The Americans had already named their coaching staff for 1984, and even though my gymnasts were the number one and two members of the team, officially I could not be there.

But Mike Jacki, the executive director of the U.S.G.F., suggests that maybe I can get an equipment-manager accreditation from AMF, the official gymnastics equipment supplier for the 1984 Games. That will allow me to be present on the floor at the Olympics, and he will help me to get it.

Regarding the Olympic preparation, I had a few different opinions than the national team coaching staff. I considered it was a major mistake to have the trials almost two months before the Games and then send the gymnasts to a six-week camp.

In that two months many of the qualified gymnasts can be injured, and you would not have efficient replacements for them from among the nonqualifiers because the other gymnasts would certainly slow down, if not completely stop their preparation. Why take the challenge of a hard adjustment to a new program, a new gym, new equipment, new food right in the most important period? The Russians, the Romanians, the East Germans never function in this way.

You should have your selection just before the Olympics. Take your top fifteen or twenty girls based on their national ranking, and tell them this: All of you are considered in the Olympic preparation. Do your best to be in excellent shape, upgrading your routines, polishing skills. Two weeks before the Games we will have the trials. Whoever is in the best shape at this moment will form the team and will line up at the Olympics.

That's how you get the best result for your country, no question about it. Anyway, when we get to Los Angeles for the training period just before the Games, we stick to our program. Mary Lou and Julianne are working with me, and the rest of the girls are working with Don Peters, the American team coach.

The difference was that we were working out twice a day with a specific intensity, just as we had in Houston. If we did not do it in this way, it is easy to become distracted, to get sloppy, to lose your conditioning and become injured.

Especially for Mary Lou it was so important to follow the special, gradually increasing intensity program, with me standing close to her, spotting properly the most difficult skills, and strengthening her spirit after the injury.

I knew that Mary Lou and Julianne had to have the maximum mental and physical preparation, because I knew it would be a dog-fight with the Romanians. I knew those girls as well as I knew myself. Five members of the Romanian team I had coached. Four of them— Ecaterina Szabo, Cristina Grigoras, Lavinia Agache, and Mihaela Stanulet—had been in that hotel lobby when we defected in New York. So I knew their good parts, bad parts, everything about them. Especially Kathy.

"Do you know Szabo?" Mary Lou would ask me.

"Yes, I know," I told her. "I work around six years with her, so I know a little."

"How she look like?"

"Just like you."

I had known Kathy since she was five years old, when her father brought her to us. Very strange story, how it happened, almost unbelievable.

A group of us had been hunting in the mountains about 150 miles from our training center in Onesti. One night at the end of the trip the woodsmen there have a big feast, with food and wine and schnapps.

After some hours, around midnight, a man comes up to me. "Can I ask you something?"

"Sure," I say. "Ask anything."

"Can you look at a little girl?"

"No," I groan. "Anything but gymnastics."

Well, he brings out this little bug, the daughter of his brother, who takes tickets on one of the interurban buses. "See," the father says, "she can stand on her head."

And the little bug, flipping, lands right on the point of her head, standing like an arrow.

"Very good," I say, trying to be polite.

"She can do again," he tells me, and again she does, landing on the point of her head.

"Can you take her?" he asks me.

"Impossible," I say. "She must be six to be enrolled in our school."

"Well, can't she just be hanging around?"

"You don't understand," I explain. "There is no way. This is a special school, and she is only five."

It is hard to convince him, but finally we go back to Onesti and continue our training. And one day, without any kind of notice, the father shows up at our gym with his daughter. He has big suitcase, she has little one.

Again I tell him the situation is impossible, but he is insisting. "Wait here," I say, and go to find Martha. "The man with the little girl is here," I tell her. "No, Bela," she says. "We cannot take responsibility for a five-year-old child who is not yet in school. Is no way."

So I go back to tell the man that he must take his daughter home, and I see her sitting there sobbing, such big tears. All alone.

"Where your father is?" I ask her.

"He-he-he leave me he-he-here," she cries. Oh, no, I think, he must be here around. But he is not. What to do now? We have a competition to travel to, there is no time to resolve this problem.

So I tell our teachers and coaches to watch over this little one for a few days, and when we come back we will decide on a plan. Well, when we return our people are going crazy. This Kathy has done nothing since we left but cry and scream in Hungarian, walking from room to room in the dormitory.

What could we do? We took her to the gym, and because we have nobody of her age, she works out with our older girls. By age seven she can do the elite compulsories. By the time she is twelve, Kathy became European junior champion and one of the strongest national team members. And in 1981 the Romanian authorities change her age from 13 to 15 to make her eligible for senior competition.

So when Mary Lou asks me about Szabo, I know everything. I know she is a very powerful little kid. Ambitious, clear-minded, and as technically clean as you can be. Kathy has a finer neuromuscular coordination than Mary Lou, but Mary Lou is stronger. All in all, they are evenly matched. It is amazing, I think, and something no other coach probably ever has. To have coached two great athletes who are on the same scene at the same time, competing against each other.

In all, seven of my present or former gymnasts will be on the floor together—Mary Lou, Julianne, and five Romanian girls. And also there, but not as a competitor, will be Nadia.

Nadia has retired from gymnastics, but the Romanians had brought her along as a representative at the invitation of the Americans. I didn't even know she was there. But one day when I am working with Mary Lou and Julianne, the door of the gym opens up and a small group of Romanian people walk in. I wasn't paying attention, but suddenly there she is.

"Nadia, you sucker, what you are doing here?" I say, and we jump into each other's arms. It was nice to see her and exchange a few words.

The only time I had talked to her since we defected was in the summer of 1983 at the World University Games in Edmonton. Well, she wasn't happy then, but that is just part of the Olympic sports life. It is the special mentality of the sports or entertainment star, it doesn't matter which. When they are at the top they fly in a special but unreal dream world. They think they deserve everything and they are getting it—compliments, rewards, compensations, all of that. And as soon as the situation starts not to go that favorable, when there are not so many people around anymore, they get frustrated and disappointed and the problems start. Is just human nature, and it was not so much different with Nadia.

So now we meet in Los Angeles. There is not much time to talk, though, and there are security guards around her and the Romanian federation president standing behind. So not much has changed.

One afternoon, in fact when I am watching Mary Lou and Julianne in one of the practice gymnasiums, I hear someone speaking to me in Romanian.

"Mister Karolyi," the voice says. "I just want to let you know that this is *our* gym, and we're gonna have a closed workout."

When you don't hear for four years Romanian, it sounds strange. Then I turn around and see it is the new president of the federation, and all my memories come back.

"Listen, buddy," I say. "You know where is your gym? Back in Bucharest. *There* is your gym. This is everybody's gym right now. But if you want to work out here along with us I welcome you."

Their gymnasts were once my girls, but the Romanians were now opponents. And since I knew they would be unbelievably aggressive politically as far as the judging was concerned, I decided I had to make a balance somehow.

Several things were working in the Romanians' favor. Since they are the only Communist Bloc nation to defy the Russians' boycott and come to Los Angeles, the Americans are welcoming the Romanians like heroes, celebrating their coming here and giving them an advantage like they never got in their lives.

At the same time, I knew there was an alliance, a coalition in the Romanians' favor among the whole European group of judges. Why? Because those European gymnastics federations are making a fortune having the Romanians doing exhibition tours in their countries. So it was in the best interest of the Italians, the French, the West Germans, the English, even the Israelis to have them be Olympic champions. What I didn't expect was the reaction of the South American countries like Brazil, Peru, Venezuela, who were also supporting the Romanians. It was, I think, their jealousy of the Americans. We had a fair rapport with the Canadians, Japanese, and Australians, but the politics was still a disadvantage for us.

And so was the schedule, which had the Americans going in the early afternoon group for the compulsories. That is a very poor time to compete, because there are very few spectators and because the judges mark relatively low then, saving the higher scores for the evening session.

So I decided that I had to be very critical and try to make the Romanians feel a little bit reserved and shaky. So right after the compulsories I went out and attacked directly the Romanian judge, Julia Roterescu.

She is my age, and was at the physical education institute in Bucharest with Martha and I. She made a few major mistakes in the early session, besides underscoring badly the American girls. Her scoring I thought was outrageous, but nobody noticed. And nobody would notice unless I called the media's attention to it.

So I said that Roterescu should not be judging, that she should be making agriculture. Politically it was important to knock the Romanians back a bit and help make sure that the competition would be decided on the floor by the gymnasts.

Because I know that with Kathy and Mary Lou we will have a fantastic all-around, with two great kids offering a sensational spectacle. It would be a great moment in Olympic history, a battle of the tenths and hundredths going up and down with each event. A competition of the wills. A contest of the spirits.

12

MARY LOU

A Unique Opportunity

I'd been to Los Angeles before, and I'd even performed inside Pauley Pavilion, the basketball arena where the Olympic gymnastics events were going to be held. But this time the whole atmosphere was different.

The American team was staying in dormitory rooms at the University of Southern California with runners and swimmers and fencers and cyclists and thousands of athletes from all over the world.

You could walk around the campus and see people from China and Brazil and Romania and dozens of other countries who'd all been working just as long and hard as you had and who had the same dreams. And all of them were on different schedules. Some were competing on the first day, others had to wait more than a week. So the cafeteria and infirmary and game rooms were open around the clock, buses were coming and going at all hours, and there were chain-link fences and security guards everywhere to protect us.

This was the Olympic Games, which I had been dreaming about for ten years, but in some ways it wasn't much different from being at Karolyi's gym.

Our training schedule hadn't changed. It was me and Julianne McNamara and twice-a-day workouts with Bela pushing us hard. Except that it was a lot more complicated, because Bela wasn't an

138

official U.S. team coach and didn't have the necessary credentials to get into the village.

So we'd get up in the morning, walk outside the gate, and see Bela waiting for us in a little car to take us to a practice gym. Then at night we'd practice with the rest of the team. It was a little unusual, but I thought it was only right that you have your own coach, the one you've been working with for two years. Besides, what we'd been doing for training was totally different.

Julianne and I were used to double workouts, because we'd been doing them for months at Karolyi's. The other girls weren't. Before we'd moved into the village we'd been out near Los Angeles for a few weeks at the team training camp at the SCATS gym. They'd tried double workouts, but it didn't work too well. You can't just switch from one a day to two; it takes two or three weeks to get your body used to the change.

Bela and Don simply had different coaching techniques. The rest of the team wasn't going to do Bela's schedule, and we weren't going to do theirs. So everybody went their own way. Where the other girls would do two bar routines, Julianne and I would do six. But things seemed to work pretty well. Bela and Don got along okay, at least around us. But Bela was still my coach, and I took his advice on everything. Like, we wanted to walk around the village and talk to all the other athletes, but Bela had told us specifically: "Go home and rest. I don't want to see you wandering everywhere." So that's what we did. Julianne and I would get up, go to workout for an hour or two in the morning, and come back and eat a little bit and rest. Then we'd go back in the evening for our second workout, eat something afterwards, maybe read a book, then go to bed.

So I never saw much of the Romanians, but I'm not sure I would have anyway. They were in the same village as we were, but you never saw them anywhere. You didn't even see the Romanians in the cafeteria. When you did see them, they weren't very friendly. I guess that's what they're told to be. They don't show their emotion that much and they're really into themselves, rather than sharing it with other people. I figured that was just the Romanian style, at least at major competitions.

I'd competed against Lavinia Agache and little Laura Cutina, yet I didn't know Ecaterina Szabo at all. But Bela had told me about her.

"She is just like you," he said. "You have same weaknesses, same strengths. Oh, it will be tough."

So I was kind of prepared for Szabo, and I was glad she was there. She was about the only top world gymnast I hadn't competed against. Either at American Cup or Chunichi Cup I'd beaten Natalia Yurchenko, Boriana Stoyanova, Maxi Gnauck, Hana Ricna, and Agache. Because of the boycott none of them were at Los Angeles. If the Romanians hadn't come, I don't think the Games would have been anything. We would have run away with it all. So I was excited about going up against them.

That's why I was glad that we were competing during the first week of the Games. I would have died if we'd just sat and waited. Because we were in the middle of the atmosphere. The swimming and diving was going on right outside my bedroom window, medals were being awarded. I'm like, Oh, gosh, we go tomorrow. I had to force my mind off it.

I kept thinking, Nine years I've worked, and this is the time where it all counts. And yet it was only another competition. I'd done those routines thousands of times. It was just a matter of doing them one more time.

Everything had gone real good in practice that week. Vaults were sticking, bars were swinging, and beam I felt very confident on. Floor, you can never tell. It's a question of adrenalin. But I was so positive, and Bela was so positive, that I just had a feeling.

I wasn't thinking much about winning the all-around; I was just shooting for some kind of medal there. I knew about the Chinese, that they were a good strong team but nothing outstanding, nothing dynamic. Ma Yanhong was great on bars, but her floor and vault weren't anything special. It was obvious that Szabo was the one to beat.

Her vault was pretty strong—she'd won a silver medal at the 1983 world championships—but I thought mine went a lot higher and further. We were pretty close on bars and floor. And her beam was solid; that's Szabo's best event.

So I knew it would come down to performance and judging. I was aware of some of the judges like Julia Roterescu of Romania. "She is very favorable to them, her little chickies," Bela told me. I guess it was only reasonable that the Romanian judge would score the Romanian kids higher, and I also expected that she might score me a 9.9 where the Americans would give me a 10. That's why I was glad that Bela was on the scene to help me strategically. He has a lot of political ability, and the judges are a little intimidated by him. But I wasn't sure exactly what he'd be trying to do.

What worried me more was that we were going earlier in the day for the compulsories on Monday. In gymnastics the judges award lower scores in the afternoon, and begin raising them at night when the better gymnasts usually perform. And both the Chinese and Romanians were going at night.

Szabo's gonna kill me in the compulsories, I thought. She's in the last rotation, they're going to raise the scores. Heck, I'm gonna have no chance.

One thing in my favor was that I was last up in every event but bars, where Julianne was the best. That meant that if I performed well I'd probably get the highest score on the American team.

It works this way. In compulsories and optionals you perform by team with the weakest girl on each apparatus going first and the best one last. The first few provide a base to build scores on, setting the stage for the last one who, at the Olympics, should be getting 9.9s and 10s.

The coaches figured I was the best candidate for a gold in the all-around, so they planted me last in vault, floor, and beam. I was legitimately the best on vault and floor, but in beam they did me a favor. That event was my life. If I could stay on the beam and have a decent routine, I knew I had a shot.

Well, I had a good day in compulsories, and I did what I thought was the best floor routine in my life. A lot of gymnasts keep to themselves or are rather stern when they do the floor exercise, but not me. It helps me to hear the crowd. It gets me going, especially on a tumbling pass. I'll be doing a dance in the corner and trying to catch my breath and get ready to go. And I'll have told Julianne and the other girls to yell and scream when I begin my tumbling pass, because that pumps me up even more.

When I finished, the crowd at Pauley Pavilion was yelling "Ten, ten, ten," but the judges shot up a 9.95. It still put me in first place going into the evening, but I knew that wouldn't last.

So Julianne and I went back at night and sat and watched. We saw nothing dynamic but the Romanians were hitting everything solid, getting 9.7s, 9.8s, 9.9s, and that builds up the scores. Then Szabo got a 10 in her floor exercise, and that was the difference. It tied her with Agache for first place, with me five-hundredths of a point behind them in second. But I was still pretty optimistic because I figured Szabo would have more of a lead on me after compulsories. When we came back Wednesday night we'd all be on the floor at the same time, going head to head.

Going into the optionals the Romanians led us by forty-five hundredths of a point, but since the American men had beaten the Chinese, who were world champions, for the gold medal the night before, we thought anything could happen.

We started out on bars, the Romanians on vault. When one of us would be going, so would one of them. So the scores would change every minute. Simona Pauca got a 9.6 for them, Pam Bileck a 9.6 for us. Cristina Grigoras got a 9.9 for them, Kathy Johnson a 9.8 for us. I got a 9.9, and Szabo came up with a 10. Then Julianne had the best bars routine of her life, and got the first 10 by any American woman in Olympic history.

So we went up on beam with really high hopes, and I'm still not sure what happened there. Pam started off really solid with a 9.6 on her weakest event. But then Michelle Dusserre wobbled, had to grab the bottom of the beam to keep from falling, and got a 9.4.

Then Tracee Talavera, who's a great beamer, went to her knees on the dismount, and wound up with a 9.15. That's how it happens on beam sometimes. Somebody is shaky and it gets contagious.

Then Kathy was given only a 9.6 on a strong routine because Roterescu marked her low, and everything stopped for seven minutes while the judges argued about it.

Meanwhile Julianne had to stand around waiting to go on, trying to stay loose and keep her concentration. That had to be the reason why she fell off right at the beginning, and ended up with a 9.2.

I wound up with the best score of all, a 9.75, and I took a little hop on my dismount. So that really put us in a hole with floor and vault coming up. Julianne got another 10 on floor, and myself and Michelle both got 9.9s, but the Romanians murdered us on beam. Pauca got a 10, Szabo a 9.95. Even though I got a 10 on vault, and Julianne and Tracee each received 9.9s, there was no way to catch up.

So the Romanians beat us for the team title by a full point, and the beam was the difference.

But it was still the best finish any American women had ever made in the Olympics, and the first medal since 1948 when the United States won a bronze, and the competition wasn't nearly as strong as it is now.

We'd made a lot of progress since 1976, when the Americans finished sixth as a team, didn't have any score better than 9.75, didn't qualify anyone higher than twenty-fourth in the all-around, and didn't have anyone in an event final. This time, we got three 10s in the optionals, qualified two girls for each of the four event finals, and had a good chance for two medals in the all-around.

And going into the weekend—the all-around finals on Friday night and the event finals on Sunday—I was right where I wanted to be. In fact, I was in a better position than I'd ever dreamed I'd be. I was the only gymnast at the Games who'd qualified for all four event finals, even beam, which must have amazed Martha. I was leading Szabo by fifteen-hundredths of a point in the all-around; she had landed on her face after her bars routine, and gotten a 9.3. And I'd be competing before a sellout crowd in my own country. That is what Bela had been talking about all those months.

Now it all came down to one night, with me and Szabo fighting it out. I remembered lying on the floor back in Fairmont in 1976, watching Nadia and thinking how lucky she was. Now, eight years later, my moment had come.

NINE YEARS,
ONE MOMENT

Before she dropped off to sleep inside the Olympic Village Thursday night, Mary Lou did what she always did before a major competition—mindscripted it completely. She mentally ran through each routine, every move, imagining everything done perfectly.

It didn't matter that this was the Olympic all-around final, nine years of work compressed into one night. The routines hadn't changed; Mary Lou could do them in her dreams. If you were completely prepared physically and mentally, as she was, there was no reason why the Olympics had to be any different than the Emerald Cup.

If you thought it was different, if you dumped the whole-world-is-watching burden on your own shoulders, then it would be difficult, and it would work to your disadvantage, paralyzing you before you even walked out there. The best approach was the unpressured one. "This is just another competition," Mary Lou told herself. "You've done these routines a thousand times. It's just a matter of doing them one more time."

Yet the difference, in the atmosphere and what was at stake, was undeniable. Pauley Pavilion, where UCLA played basketball, was filled to capacity with nine thousand people who'd paid at least $95 to get inside. Some of them—the ones who'd been holding plaintive NEED TICKETS signs outside—had paid as much as five times that.

Gymnastics, both men's and women's, had become the hottest ticket at the Games and the featured attraction on ABC's prime-time telecast. And Friday night's women's all-around, which would decide the best gymnast, was its centerpiece. One routine on each apparatus, joined with fifty percent of the preliminary score to make up the total.

The top thirty-six finishers from the compulsory and optional exercises earlier in the week had qualified, but it was a two-woman duel and everybody in Los Angeles knew it. Retton versus Szabo.

"Well, at least she's about my size," Mary Lou mused, hours before they marched out onto the floor. "We're both about four foot nine. I've seen her work, and she's terrific. But what she doesn't know about me is that I'm tougher than she is."

Mary Lou had other advantages. She would be performing on familiar ground, surrounded by partisan spectators ready to help push her toward glory. The home-court advantage, and all the friendly distractions that came with it, weren't necessarily a benefit, Karolyi had said. But Mary Lou wanted the support and the adrenalin it would stir up in her.

She viewed her lead—fifteen-hundredths of a point—as an unexpected bonus. She'd figured Szabo would have been in front coming into the final. The odds had shifted in her favor now. "We're bettin' on Retton," read a sign in the stands.

"I'm going to show these people I can win it," Mary Lou decided. "America has never won a thing in women's gymnastics. If I can do it, these people are going to go crazy."

The rotation, the order in which the gymnasts compete on each apparatus, would be against her early in the evening. Szabo's two best events—beam and floor—came up first. Mary Lou's best ones—floor and vault—came last.

"She'll be ahead, you'll be ahead, she'll be ahead, you'll be ahead," Karolyi had told her. "You will fight it out that way."

Mary Lou would also fight it out alone. Karolyi was not a member of the U.S. coaching staff. The only reason he was on the floor at all was because he'd been able to cadge an equipment-mover's credential from AMF. And even then he had restricted access, limited to a narrow photographers' pen behind a waist-high barrier. He could speak to Mary Lou if she came over to him; otherwise he had to communicate by eye contact and simple hand signals.

None of them could tell Mary Lou anything more than what she already knew. They could reaffirm and inspire, but that was all. The gymnast had to do it herself. If Mary Lou won a medal, she would have to accomplish it on her own. If she wobbled, slipped, fell, or failed, she was alone. Victory, defeat, and anything in between depended on what Mary Lou Retton could make happen in perhaps six minutes in the spotlight.

When she lined up for the entering ceremony that began the evening, Mary Lou was the leader, but she knew that would change quickly, maybe even after the first rotation.

"Beam's Szabo's best event," she realized. "She'll stick it—a 9.95, even a 10. No way she's gonna fall. And there's no way bars is a 10 routine for me."

Szabo, after all, had been doing tricks on beam since she was five. For her an Olympic routine was no more difficult than walking along a curbstone. So she came out crisp and calm, head cocked expectantly, waiting for the signal to begin. Her long curly brown hair was tied into a ponytail with white yarn. Her eyes were shaded with blue makeup. There was no tension in that face, not even a trace of doubt.

Nobody in the building could manage what Szabo nailed cleanly every day in workout—four back handsprings in a row, measured off precisely, executed seamlessly. Szabo knew that, Mary Lou knew that, and Karolyi knew that, too. So he'd given Mary Lou the same admonition he'd been giving his girls for twenty years: Don't watch anybody else. Just worry about yourself. And don't even look at your own score.

"But I *have* to look at her," Mary Lou told herself. "It's only human." So she watched Szabo get up safely and cleanly with a straddle press mount, which set the tone for the whole routine.

There would not be a single reckless move, nothing that might disturb the sense of alert command that Szabo wanted to project for ninety seconds four feet up.

She easily ran through the first two skills—a handstand and a planche—then walked to the front end of the beam to set up for the back handsprings. Bing-bing-bing-bing, Szabo knocked them off, finishing with a flourish and inches to spare. Then she polished off the rest—back handspring, back layout, back walkover, leaps, turns, split—as though the apparatus were four feet wide, a Bucharest boulevard, and Szabo were out for an agreeable Sunday promenade.

"Romanian girls know how to walk on the beam," Martha Karolyi had said, and it was true. Szabo's dismount—a double back somersault—was a formality, a signature. "Ten," Mary Lou conceded, and got up to approach the chalk bowl and the bars.

It *was* a 10, and Szabo knew it the moment she touched ground. Her mouth blossomed into a giddy smile, and she waved and blew kisses to the crowd, whose affection she clearly hoped to win. When the score went up, she threw a fist in the air.

"That," the gesture said, "is a Szabobeam." Mary Lou, shaking her arms loose like a boxer might, waiting for the green light and the go-ahead, put on the Retton game face. Jaw set, eyes clear and focused, lips pressed taut.

Coincidentally, "Eye of the Tiger," the theme music from *Rocky III*, was playing for somebody's floor routine. It was terrific stuff to psych up to, but the boxing simile went only so far.

Boxing was a true one-on-one duel. You won by making your opponent lose. It was a judged sport, but you could render the judging and any possibility of bias moot by applying a knockout punch. You had no such alternative in gymnastics. You could pick out your archrival and issue some sort of challenge to her, spoken or not. But the judges made the decision.

You had no control over that, and even less control over your opponent. You could not screech like a howler monkey to distract her on beam. You couldn't sow carpet tacks on the vault runway or tweak her ankle when she was switching bars. If she was perfect, you had to be perfect. So the true competition was with yourself and your imperfections.

Szabo was peforming at different times on different events, literally on the other side of the floor. Mary Lou could watch her, make mental note of the score, but it was trivia. She had to make it happen for herself, and she had to begin on the uneven parallel bars.

"Control yourself up there," Mary Lou thought. "Swing and stretch. Do things *longer*." It would probably not earn a 10, but the routine had to be strong. If she conceded more than a tenth of a point, Szabo would draw even.

Her mount—a half-twist to the high bar—was solid. Mary Lou arched her body into a perfectly good handstand, then came down and under and up into a release move, a reverse Hecht. That meant letting go of the bar as she came over the top and catching it on her way down on the other side. It was a tricky skill that involved clearing the bar with both legs, and Mary Lou's knees bent slightly midway through.

Nothing serious. "Arms, Arms," Karolyi shouted. "Long. . . guud. . . powerful." Mary Lou was back in control now, her giant swing flawless. She swung again on the high bar, building up momentum for the Retton Flip, her bars trademark that was designed to leave her sitting up high in a look-ma-no-hands pose.

She came down for a belly-beat off the low bar to set it up, but wound up perched just a tad uneasily on the high one. If they hadn't taken off five-hundredths for the bent knees on the reverse Hecht, they might there.

Now she'd gone under and up and into a peach-basket without leaving the high bar, hanging on upside-down and inside-out. From there it was straight to a handstand on the low bar, then back to the high one to prepare for the front half with a pike dismount.

It was a flying-squirrel move that began with both hands and feet on the bar, flung you under the high bar and over the low one, then put you through a half-twist before you landed it. Mary Lou went through it without a hitch, getting her hips wonderfully high on the twist—but didn't quite stick. The judges couldn't help but notice a backward hop on the landing, and Karolyi grimaced.

"Pretty guuud," he told Mary Lou when she bounded over to check in, but he guessed it wouldn't be good enough. As the crowd growled and hooted the judges, the board flashed 9.85. Szabo had pulled alongside in a single rotation.

Okay, Mary Lou thought, as she stripped off her hand grips and began pondering the beam. I will fight even harder. If everything went to form, she'd be behind after the next rotation, and she was braced for that, too.

Szabo was world champion on floor, and she'd stuffed her Olympic routine full of star-spangled music to charm an American audience. A 10 was not impossible. Mary Lou had improved greatly, but she did not have a Szabobeam and didn't pretend to. Still, she had to get a 9.8 or risk being out of contention before the evening was half complete.

So while she waited her turn, Mary Lou simulated her beam routine seven, eight, nine times on the floor until Karolyi told her to quit. "Stop now," he muttered. "You rest."

So she sat back to observe Szabo's Yankee Doodle Dandy of a floor exercise, with "An American in Paris," "Rhapsody in Blue," "Dixie," and "The Battle Hymn of the Republic" all blended together and served up by synthesizer. She's really Americanized it, Mary Lou thought, but she knew that the important thing was the tumbling. If Szabo came sloppily out of a pass, if knees buckled and feet gave way, it would shave off a tenth of a point, and that might make the difference.

She began with a daring full-in double back, and semibotched it, landing with her shoulders low and feet wobbly, and had to take a giant step to steady herself. Something had to be deducted there. Otherwise it was a terrific floor exercise, full of ballet moves and brio and intricate tumbling, scarce on filler. For her second pass Szabo strung together a roundoff back handspring, a one-and-a-half twist, another handspring, and another one-and-a-half twist, and finished with a punch front flip that took her across the mat in two blinks of the eye. But where she usually chose another full-in for her finale, this time Szabo ended with a simpler roundoff back handspring double back. She did that just to be safe, and it made sense.

Szabo's routine had been crammed with enough action as it was, decorated with graceful touches, and the crowd had loved it, Gershwin and all. Nine-nine-five, the judges said, and Szabo ran off the floor delighted.

You're not going to get a 10, Mary Lou concluded as she considered her next apparatus. Maybe a 9.9. Just do your best.

The beam, she had told herself for weeks, is your life. You can't win the all-around without it. Fall or have a major break, and it's over. Because Szabo won't mess up.

Mary Lou was fairly certain that she wouldn't, either. Her beams had been solid all week, the best on the American team. The quivering premonitions she once had had, the sense of impending crash landings every time she went up, had been buried long ago. She could do eight beam routines in a row in the gym, with Martha inspecting every one, and make them all whistle-clean. No reason why she couldn't do another one here.

Mary Lou's mount—a stag-leap—was steady, her early turns flawless. A handstand was totally controlled, and her back walkover, back tuck right on the money. Nothing wrong so far, and as Mary Lou leaped her way back to the other end she could hear Karolyi shouting "Yes!"

Time for the front flip, which seemed to be fine until she had to bring herself up out of it. Then she felt herself wobbling, her feet turning her body sideways, and had to overcompensate with her arms to right herself. There was no way to disguise it. Take off a tenth.

More leaps now, all of them sure. "Not too bad," Karolyi mumbled. Then a back flip—and a slight wobble. Not nearly as pronounced and well concealed.

Still, with the routine nearly done, there'd been no major break in it, none of the here-we-go flailing that usually prefaced a fall. All Mary Lou needed to do now was nail the dismount, a double back somersault, and it would be a remarkably clean routine.

When she did, Mary Lou felt exuberance sweep through her. Yeah! she thought. I can let loose now. I can *go*. I'm over the hump.

Back on the sidelines she accepted congratulations, grinned with relief, took two deep breaths and let the air out in a whoosh, then sat down anxiously to await the score. When it came—9.8—Karolyi groaned. "It is killed," he murmured. "It is over. Arrgghhh. The Italian judge has got a deal with the Romanians."

Mary Lou raised resigned eyebrows, and swallowed hard. "Can't sulk about it," she decided. "Just go on to the next one."

It had been the best beam routine of her life. Whether it deserved better than a 9.8 was irrelevant now, and Mary Lou realized that. You did your best and the judges decided your fate. That was how gymnastics operated, and always would.

Now came Karolyi, his pessimism shelved. Maybe Mary Lou had only a flickering chance at the gold medal, but he couldn't let her think that. Besides, as long as there was a mathematical chance, there was a practical chance. This was, after all, an athletic event involving human beings. Two nights before, Szabo had fallen flat on her face. No reason why that couldn't happen again.

"It is all right," Karolyi was saying. "You have to work now like you have never worked in your life. Okay? Never."

Mary Lou, her eyes glistening, nodded, bit her lip, and tried to smile.

"Hey, it's going to be all right, I tell you," Karolyi said.

"Okay," Mary Lou said, and sat down to think. Two rotations down, two to go, with Szabo leading by fifteen-hundredths of a point. But Szabo's best events were behind her now, and Mary Lou's were still ahead. If momentum had been in the Romanian's favor, it was no longer, and Mary Lou knew that.

For me, a 10 on floor is not out of the question, she figured. I've done it before. I just have to go full-strength, not hold back, and hope the scoring is good. And hope they don't mark Szabo too high on the vault.

Mary Lou was concerned about that. Szabo's vault—a full-twisting Tsukahara in the pike position—wasn't nearly as daring as Mary Lou's layout, and it went nowhere near as high or as far. But the judges had given her a 10 for it during the team competition. If Szabo reaped another one now, it was over. Period.

Pretty slim chances for me, Mary Lou suspected. I need two 10s, and she's got to lose two-tenths somewhere. Well, if it has to be, a silver's not too bad. It's pretty.

But Szabo would have to earn her gold, and Mary Lou was determined to apply as much psychological pressure as she could. Compared to Mary Lou's charge down the runway, which was not unlike a bulldozer in overdrive, Szabo's approach was a timid canter. It had none of the full-tilt, I-don't-care sprint or the punch that flung Mary Lou skyward.

Halfway through the twist on her first vault Szabo's legs began coming apart. It was an early-warning signal. When she landed, her feet spread outward like Charlie Chaplin's. "No-no-no," Karolyi would have growled at her. "Sloppy."

But the judges still gave Szabo a 9.9. She's going to stick her second one, Mary Lou thought, and it'll be over.

The rules said that the better of the two vaults would count. But on the second Szabo's knees were splayed even more, her legs pointing at different parts of the Pauley Pavilion ceiling. When she touched down Szabo took a bunny-hop forward that might as well have been a Carl Lewis long jump.

Nine-eight-oh, the scoreboard said. Suddenly there was a sliver of daylight.

"Don't hold back," Karolyi urged, as Mary Lou put her blank game face back on and prepared to take to the floor. "Go for it. You have nothing to lose."

Nobody needed to tell her that. With the bars and beam behind her, you couldn't have held Mary Lou back with a shoulder harness. Her final two events called for strong legs and a sense of abandon, and she had been born with both.

If Szabo had defined a beam routine à la 1984, Mary Lou had put her stamp on the floor exercise. Slow violins, pique turns, and ponytails were déclassé. The Retton floor was power and energy and adrenalin, and it was performed anywhere from four inches to four feet above terra firma.

And the music—a 1930s tune called "Johnny, My Friend"—was taken right from the Romanian master file on audience participation. You could not help but clap to it, and Geza Poszar had choreographed sharps and poses and motion that helped transform Mary Lou into a dervish, a dynamo.

"It fits you like a glove," Karolyi had said a hundred times, and Mary Lou agreed. Now that floor routine might just be the stuff from which gold medals were cast.

The tumbling would be no problem; it was in the genes. What Mary Lou had to do was forge an emotional bond with nine thousand Americans. "Be a lady now," Karolyi reminded her just before she went out to assume her starting pose.

Everything would depend on the first tumbling pass, a double layout that would bring Mary Lou from corner to corner. Nobody else at the Games could match it for raw height, and nobody could stick it so securely. If she hit it, Mary Lou knew she would electrify the crowd and supercharge herself, and momentum could take her from there. When she did, the game face vanished, replaced by The Smile. "You've got to show it off," Mary Lou told herself. "Show the people. Show the judges."

So she grinned and spun and went up on tiptoe, bounced and flexed and grinned again. "*Look* at the people," Karolyi was calling. "Contact. Smiling. Faces. *Faces.*"

Now the second tumbling pass—a full-in double back, followed by a front flip. Blam, solid. It was a marvelous floor exercise, anchored firmly by the tumbling, which was pumping electrons into everything else.

Now more contact, more faces, a chance for the lungs to refill, everything done with bravura and juice. And the final pass—a round-off back handspring double tuck that plunked her down with authority where she had started.

Nobody had to tell Mary Lou how it had gone. ABC commentator Jack Whitaker, though, informed several hundred million people. "Mary Lou, how *do* you do?" he concluded. "If she were a tourist attraction, she'd be Niagara Falls."

From his holding area Karolyi, his mustache quivering with excitement, whacked his palms impatiently on the barrier. "No way they don't give a ten," he kept saying. "There is no way. It is the best floor routine ever done. That is the perfection."

The judges seemed to be taking forever. "Come *onnn*," Mary Lou muttered, waiting for the score to flash. Then the numbers shimmered, and the crowd went wild.

"YES!" Mary Lou shrieked, threw both arms up to salute the 10, and went back out on the floor to milk it, to play to the spectators, to rev up the emotion for the final rotation.

Karolyi, despondent only moments before, was now emitting Transylvanian war whoops. "That's it, that's it, little buddy," he shouted. "Fantastic."

Then he swooped her up into a bear hug that left Mary Lou's size-three feet twenty-four inches above the ground. The building had come alive now, with American flags sprouting everywhere and ticketholders chanting, "U-S-A, U-S-A."

Szabo's lead had been whittled to five-hundredths of a point. If Szabo's bars routine wasn't perfect, Mary Lou would have a piece of Szabo's gold medal. If Szabo was off by only a tenth, Mary Lou would have it all. Nobody else was involved. Szabo's teammate Simona Pauca had held off Julianne McNamara for the bronze. It was lioness versus lioness now, lesser take the silver. Precisely the way Mary Lou liked it.

Cryptic expressions along the Romanian bench, where teammates were offering Szabo some final words of advice and patting her on the shoulder before she went to chalk up.

Mary Lou was pacing her own sideline, glancing over at Szabo, trying to catch her eye to let her know it was going to be a showdown.

The crowd couldn't help you now. Your coach couldn't help you. Your teammates, friends, family, the TV commentators, the spectators couldn't either. The gymnast had to get up on bars or approach the vaulting horse alone. If her knees buckled or her hands slipped, it was her problem, her solution, her loss, her victory.

So Szabo chalked up, went over to adjust the low bar, and stood waiting for the green light. Alone. When it came, she began with a vault over the low bar to the high one, went to a giant, then a handstand to a release move.

So far the routine was above reproach. Bars was Szabo's weakest apparatus, but weak relative to what? She had still shared the silver medal with teammate Lavinia Agache at the 1983 world championships. At this level weakness was calculated in hundredths of points.

Szabo was on the low bar now, executing a one-and-a-half twist. Suddenly it began to get away from her. Her hands fumbled for a hold, her body uncomfortably close to the end of the bar and the guy wire. Her teeth clenched together as she struggled to retain control. Nothing serious. Unless you were watching in slow motion the semislip was barely noticeable. But after fifteen seconds of certainty and command, it was enough to throw Szabo off-center.

She recovered in a millisecond, came under the bar with a double leg shoot-through, and went up top to build up speed for the dismount, a double flyaway. If she stuck it, it was probably a 9.95, which would be good for a share of the gold medal, no matter what Mary Lou did.

Mary Lou was still walking her sideline, twenty-five steps in one direction, turn, twenty-five steps in the other. It might have looked like a nervous stomach, but it wasn't. She wasn't pacing, she was stalking.

Karolyi had told her to ignore Szabo, but Mary Lou would not. She was inspecting her rival's routine for any sign of a break, any flaw that would lead a judge to shave off a tenth. At this point the smallest error would be just as damaging to Szabo as an on-your-head pratfall.

Szabo had released now, and was into a somersault, then a second one. She landed, then took a giant step back with her left foot. You could see it from the twentieth row of Pauley Pavilion. You could see it even if you couldn't tell a handstand from a handbasket.

There it is, Mary Lou thought. You can do it. You can *do* it. All she had wanted was the tiniest crack, the smallest bit of breathing space. Now Szabo had given it to her.

The judges couldn't ignore that step—9.9. Still, Szabo guessed it might be good enough. The Romanian team was exuberant. Pauca came over to Szabo grinning, and Szabo thrust her right fist firmly into the air as if to say: Got it!

Behind the barrier Karolyi did some quick mental arithmetic, then gave the numbers to Mary Lou—9.95 to tie, 10 to win.

"Run strong," he told her. "Then, *bang*, hit it. Then high. Okay? Strong, bang, high, okay?"

"Okay," Mary Lou nodded.

"Bang, okay?"

"Okay."

She had plenty of time to ponder it. Szabo had gone up first in her group on bars, but several vaulters—Romania's Laura Cutina, Canada's Bonnie Wittmeier, Great Britain's Natalie Davis—were scheduled ahead of Mary Lou.

So she just kept walking, swinging her arms, staying loose and cool, waiting for her moment.

"Relax," Karolyi said. "The biggest vault in the world. And stick it. Okay, little buddy?"

No problem. She had done this vault hundreds of times. Mary Lou could break the full-twisting layout Tsukahara down into a thousand separate freeze-frames—run, hit the board, punch off, twist, land. She could do it blindfolded, do it if you dragged her out of bed with the Spillers' house bisected by a tree, put her out into the center of Baltic Street, and had her throw the vault in the middle of a tornado.

It didn't matter that nine years of training had come down to four seconds. Nothing so big in Mary Lou's life had ever depended on something so small. There were a dozen things that could go wrong, and any one of them would separate her from the gold.

But nothing was going to go wrong. Her preparation and her personality did not allow for that possibility. Technically, her Sook was clean. Physically, she was in perfect condition. Mentally, she relished the challenge. Everything she had done since her first day at Monica's Dance Studio had pointed toward this moment. There was no chance she wouldn't hit the vault. It hadn't been mindscripted that way.

"Now or never, okay?" Karolyi urged as Mary Lou walked to the top of the runway and stepped in a puddle of spilled Coca-Cola. It might have unnerved somebody else. Not Mary Lou, and certainly not now. "No problem," somebody assured her. "It'll make you stick."

When she took her position exactly 73.5 feet from the horse, everything inside Pauley Pavilion came to a stop. Everybody watched. Szabo could do nothing; her evening was through. Half of the planet was tuned into the Olympic Games, and for this moment, in Bucharest, in Moscow, in Berlin, in a small Romanian coal-mining town called Vulcan, in a small West Virginia coal-mining town called Fairmont, they were watching one sixteen-year-old American girl.

Mary Lou seemed unaware of any of that. She was at the center of a full building on a warm August night in Los Angeles with TV lights focused on her face, but she wasn't perspiring. Everything anywhere else was irrelevant. All that mattered was a stationary piece of padded wood that had to be surmounted. And the piece of wood couldn't move. Mary Lou would win the gold medal, share it, or lose it entirely on her own.

She spat in her hands and rubbed them together—for luck or traction or both. She jogged quickly in place to loosen her legs, then anointed her hands again.

When the green light came on Mary Lou peered down the runway at the horse, glanced down to make her takeoff spot, then looked up and stared at the horse. The building was so quiet that you could hear photographers' motor-drives humming.

When she began her approach, Mary Lou exploded like a sprinter coming out of the blocks, teeth gritted, arms pumping, legs churning. She was eleven years old again, leading the field in the Hershey's national fifty-yard dash.

She bounded onto the springboard, punched off aggressively and went vertical, bent for hyperspace. Her body was aligned flawlessly in full amplitude with legs together at every point—toes, ankles, knees, thighs.

It was the layout Tsukahara as only one woman in the world could perform it, and Mary Lou had plenty of time and space to execute the twist. I've got it, she thought in midair, with her ankles suspended somewhere over her shoulders. All she had to do was stick, which she did. So solid, as she was fond of saying, that she shook the arena. Mary Lou didn't need to look over at the judges or wait for their score. Perfect. Both her arms went up, like a referee signaling a touchdown.

As the crowd leaped to its feet to render an ovation, Mary Lou clapped her hands and went over to embrace Karolyi, who had come over the barrier with a vault of his own.

Peters, who said he was afraid that the judges would penalize Mary Lou for Karolyi's being on the floor without proper credentials, came over quickly to shoo him away.

"Don't worry about," Karolyi told him. Nothing could change what Mary Lou had done. *Sports Illustrated* would call it "A Vault Without Fault."

"Olympic champion," Karolyi shouted. "There's a ten. There's a ten. Fantastic, fantastic."

The crowd was calling for the 10 now. When it came up Mary Lou threw her fist in the air, clapped her hands again, and began laughing, tossing her head back and looking at the ceiling and beyond. *Did* it! her face said.

There was no way to improve on it, and no need to. But Mary Lou wanted to duplicate the vault in her second attempt. To honor her rivals, to honor the judges, to honor the competition. And to show the world that it had been no fluke. That she could do it two, three, six, a dozen times, just as she did every day in the gym.

Before the crowd had a chance to settle, before the enormity of what she had done had sunk into her mind, Mary Lou was poised at the end of the runway again, spitting into her hands, raising her arm, going for it.

The second vault was a carbon-copy of the first one from initial step to landing. If anything, it was stuck even more firmly. Another 10. Mary Lou ran back to Karolyi for a series of bear hugs and whoops. "Unbelievable, little buddy," he exulted. "We did it."

Mary Lou was beyond words now. All she could do was laugh and shake her fist and laugh some more. There had never been a moment remotely like it in gymnastics history. An American teenager who'd been on her national team for only fourteen months had won the Olympic all-around title by five one-hundredths of a point by nailing her last two routines for perfect scores.

And the way it had ended, with a blur and a thunderclap, brought 9,000 people up out of their seats, mouths agape. Mary Lou was bounding from one end of the building to the other now, propelled by a spontaneous roar of surprise and delight from the stands that began as soon as she touched down and was still reverberating.

It was an American crowd, responding to the kind of moment Americans loved. They were a country of dreamers and gamblers, brought up to believe that anything was possible. If the seventies had made them doubt that, one of their own teenagers had just restored their faith.

Mary Lou had turned fate on its head simply because she believed she could and dared to try. As tribute, an American flag was being readied somewhere in Pauley Pavilion and a gold medal was being unboxed. And still, the cheering went on.

This is like a fairy tale, Mary Lou thought. All the hard work, all the injuries, all the sweat and pain were worth it.

Six weeks earlier her knee had been swollen double, the odds against her winning a medal of any kind cranked up a hundred to one. Fifteen minutes earlier she had all but been consigned to the silver, facing numbers that all went in Szabo's favor.

Now, on the Romanian side, Lavinia Agache glumly threw an arm around Szabo's shoulders to console her. While thousands of flashbulbs sought Mary Lou's face, while photographers and cameramen came up close and bore in, her rival pulled on her red-and-white warmup suit, sat down by herself, and bowed her head.

She had come from fifteen-hundredths of a point down at the beginning of the evening to lead by that much midway through. Her teammates and coaches had told her she was home free, and she had begun to believe it. Szabo had scored a 10 on the beam, and had no individual mark below 9.90. But it had not been good enough.

When she brought her head up, Szabo's eyes were wet but her face was composed. "She is tough," Karolyi had told Mary Lou. "Just like you."

Kathy Szabo was in a foreign country halfway around the world from Bucharest, performing before an audience that liked her but loved someone else. She had lost the gold medal by a fraction of a fraction, because one foot had given way once. Still, she managed a smile.

Gymnastics is a sport of quivers and microseconds and decimal points, and she accepted that. Szabo had beaten Olga Mostepanova for the world title in floor exercise by seventy-five thousandths of a point. She could find a way to live with a silver medal here.

Now Olympic officials were assembling the medalists, attendants were readying the three flags, and costumed buglers were announcing the presentation ritual with a fanfare.

Escorted by two women in white, Mary Lou emerged in her blue USA sweatsuit, followed by Szabo and Pauca, and walked to a place behind the awards stand where no American woman had ever before ventured.

The first words over the loudspeaker were in French, one of the two formal Olympic languages. They were telling Mary Lou officially that she had won, but she didn't understand them.

Then the English: "Winner of the gold medal, scoring seventy-nine point one seven five, representing the United States of America . . ."

Here I am, Mary Lou thought, watching a gymnastics federation official come forward with the gold medal and drape it around her neck. It's my time now.

A woman gave her a bouquet, which she held aloft. Then Szabo came over from the second-place level to give the customary kiss on both cheeks, followed by Pauca.

"Ladies and gentleman," a voice intoned, "please rise for the playing of the national anthem of the United States of America."

Mary Lou put her hand over her heart, watched her national flag go up between two red, yellow, and blue Romanian tricolors, and began to sing.

"This is the moment," she told herself, "I worked nine years for."

EPILOGUE

An All-American Story

The gold medal was still at her bedside when she awoke Saturday morning. Not that Mary Lou had doubted it would be; the Olympic village was only slightly less secure than SAC headquarters. Still, a tiny voice somewhere in her subconscious had hinted that it might all be a vapor, that somebody could still find a way to wipe out her victory.

Mary Lou had fretted about that in the doping room Friday night, where a nurse and several officials were waiting for her urine sample. Running down an imaginary checklist she crossed off one item after another.

She was an American citizen. She'd qualified for the team, and was wearing the appropriate credential around her neck. She was old enough to compete. The scoring mathematics were correct, the numbers had been posted by computer, and nobody was disputing them. And she hadn't used any illegal drugs.

Wait a minute, Mary Lou realized. I took some nose spray for a cold a few days ago. I've had a few aspirin. What if they show up on the machine? Can they disqualify me?

Not now, she concluded the next day. She'd already been to the press conference, had given out gold-medal statements: "Nobody thought it could be done. But you know what? I went and did it."

She'd been chauffeured around Los Angeles in a limousine, and had spent half the night talking to the television networks. Thousands of Americans were already scribbling and mailing congratulatory notes.

And the medal was still there. It was something like coming out of a dream in which you'd found a million dollars on the sidewalk and seeing the money lying at the foot of the bed. It *had* to be real.

It *was* real, and was rapidly becoming surreal. Mary Lou had ordered an Olympic ring at a bookstore next to the village. "Pick it up anytime Saturday," the man had told her. But the moment she stepped outside the gate, Mary Lou found herself engulfed by well-wishers and autograph-seekers. My God, she thought. All these people, literally overnight. Police gathered protectively around her; a teammate had to pick up the ring later.

Then, when she turned up for the customary day-after conference at the main press center downtown, Mary Lou realized that the room was jammed with hundreds of journalists waiting to record every word. "Why me?" she wondered. Swimmers Tracy Caulkins, Nancy Hogshead, and Mary T. Meagher had each won three gold medals; sprinter Valerie Brisco-Hooks would win three in the next few days.

But Mary Lou had touched a rare public chord. ABC's cameras had shown her face for days, and had focused even more tightly upon it Friday night. When the fan mail began pouring in by the boxful, that was the theme: You've been in our living room all week. We feel we know you. We love you.

How can you know me? she wondered. I don't know you. But that was irrelevant. Her last name, all but unknown to the nonsporting public a month earlier, was now superfluous. To two hundred million Americans she was Mary Lou—their sister, daughter, grandchild, girlfriend, babysitter, neighbor. All because of one night, one moment, one unexpected gold medal.

There were still chances for four more on Sunday in the apparatus finals. Karolyi, who'd spent Friday night curled up asleep in his little car in the Pauley Pavilion parking lot, because he no longer had a room, kept reminding Mary Lou about that.

"We have to get our minds back on what we came here for," he told her. Mary Lou was still favored to win the vault, had an even-money chance for a gold on the floor, and figured to medal on bars. Yet after the all-around she felt satisfied, drained.

"I know it's a terrible attitude to have," she told herself. "But I've already won the big one. Anything extra is a bonus."

Sunday belonged to Szabo, who came back to win gold medals in vault and floor, and share a third with teammate Simona Pauca on beam, and to McNamara, who posted a 10 to share the bars title with Ma, and finished second on the floor.

On another night in another year Mary Lou's finals would have made American history. Nobody else at Los Angeles had qualified for all four: Imagine *me* in an Olympic beam final, she mused.

She still came away with a silver in the vault behind Szabo, bronzes on bars and floor, and fourth place on beam. "Not bad," Mary Lou concluded. "I've got at least one of each color—a gold, two silvers, and two bronzes." Only Chinese gymnast Li Ning with six won more.

She still had a week to relish the afterglow, to roam the village, drop in on events, tell her story. But Mary Lou wanted instead to go back to Fairmont, where she'd spent exactly four days in ten months.

"Bela thinks I should get away from it all," she told her mother. "I'm going home."

She figured she could fly to Pittsburgh, take the commuter plane to the small airport at Clarksburg, and slip into Fairmont unobserved shortly before dusk on Monday.

No chance. The whole town had gone whacko after Mary Lou had won the all-around, piling into cars after midnight and pounding on horns in a dizzy downtown intersection. Everybody from politicians to supermarket checkers seemed to have deduced her itinerary and turned out to pay homage.

Governor Jay Rockefeller, who was running for U.S. Senate, was on hand to bestow a kiss and a testimonial. "You," he informed Mary Lou, "are the greatest thing ever to happen to the state of West Virginia."

A white Buick Riviera was produced forthwith, and through bleary eyes Mary Lou saw groups of fellow citizens lining the road to the interstate, which led to Fairmont and to yet another triumphal march.

This one she surveyed from inside the "cherry-picker" atop Engine Number 1, Fairmont's fire truck nonpareil, which crept for three hours toward the family home on Beverly Road, soon to be renamed Mary Lou Retton Drive.

Souvenir hunters had already made off with the mailbox, and had uprooted chunks of turf from the lawn. A brace of police officers stood sentry, a crank had already phoned in a death threat.

So Mary Lou was home, yet she knew that it would never be the same. "I'm in this house, I'm part of this family," she told herself. "But I don't live here."

The Rettons had figured she'd be gone for only eighteen months. Houston, then the Olympics, then back to Fairmont to finish high school. Now both Mary Lou and her parents sensed it would never happen.

She'd planned to spend four days at home decompressing, but before the week was over Mary Lou had returned twice to Los Angeles—once for the "Tonight Show" and a chat with Joan Rivers, then for the closing ceremonies, a laser-and-pyrotechnic display that would do until World War IX came along.

Meanwhile the mail was still rolling in from six-year-olds and sixty-year-olds and everyone in between. It came from preachers and prisoners, from the sick and the poor, and a common strain ran through all of it: Thank you. You deserved it. You inspired us. Thank you.

Americans had won eighty-three gold medals, but Mary Lou had come somehow to represent them all. "At last," wrote Bob Ottum in *Sports Illustrated*, "the average-size people of America have a heroine they can look down to."

Mary Lou was the Olympian who stood on tiptoe and fit the President for a scarlet U.S. team blazer. ("Can she reach you?" Nancy Reagan wondered.) When the U.S. Olympic Committee brought its 221 medalists on a five-city tour, she was its centerpiece. Thousands of Washingtonians stood in the rain along Pennsylvania Avenue, calling her name.

When New York threw its first ticker-tape parade since the hostages returned from Iran, Mary Lou strolled arm-in-arm with Mayor Ed

Koch through the "Canyon of Heroes," from Battery Park to City Hall, as two million people cheered.

She was a symbol of American optimism and toughness and exuberance, and America loved her for that. In a society that urged you to Go For It, to roll the dice and dare to dream, Mary Lou had made it happen.

Now America wanted to reward her for it. Before she'd even left Los Angeles, Karolyi, who remembered how Romania had consumed another gymnast eight years earlier, began preparing Mary Lou for a tidal wave.

"We're going to have to make some adjustments now, some decisions," he told her. "You will be having many opportunities to make money, and you will have to know what to do."

Agents and other would-be representatives were already approaching en masse, pressing business cards into her hand, urging Mary Lou to call. "Sure, sure," she told them, but she was overwhelmed.

Karolyi recommended a New Yorker named John Traetta, a former gymnast who'd represented the U.S. Gymnastics Federation. Almost immediately he was handling several hundred calls a day from companies offering engagements and endorsements. Television networks, their appetites whetted in August, hungered for Mary Lou during the fall. One even offered her her own series. Traetta, concerned about overexposure and inappropriate advertising connections, proceeded deliberately. Some possibilities were rejected out of hand as unsuitable.

Mary Lou belonged on the front of a Wheaties box, where no female face had ever appeared. General Mills willingly obliged, and also featured her in a television advertisement crunching the "breakfast of champions" in between somersaults. Mary Lou did what the big boys did, the chorus testified, and the big boys had better watch out.

McDonald's, Vidal Sassoon, Dobie leisure wear, and Pony athletic shoes quickly got in line. Mary Lou was America's poster girl, and as such she quickly got to sample a string of star-spangled traditions. She was a presenter at the Emmy Awards ceremonies. She sat in a box seat at the World Series, appeared in the Macy's Thanksgiving Day parade, and performed alongside Bob Hope in his Christmas special. Gary Trudeau mentioned her in a "Doonesbury" cartoon, listing her alongside Old Glory and nuclear superiority as American heirlooms.

She had figured that by December the craziness would subside. If anything, Mary Lou realized when she ventured out, it was the opposite. Shopping, or any other public venture, had grown all but impossible. "I've got to walk with my head down and my collar up," she thought. So Mary Lou bought her Christmas gifts in Hong Kong, where more people were her size, but even there they recognized her. In Japan, crowds followed her crying, "Retton-san, Retton-san." Back in the States, The Smile gave her away.

She'd be hurrying through an airport and would hear rapid footsteps gaining on her. "Aren't you Mary Lou Retton?" someone would say. "No, I'm Sally Smith," Mary Lou would reply—then dissolve into laughter, flashing The Smile.

It was hopeless. She could not be Mary Lou and not laugh. She could not sign one autograph without being asked to sign a hundred. She could not go to a movie, a Chinese restaurant, or a baseball game without being recognized—and mobbed.

At first it puzzled her. "How can this be happening?" Mary Lou wondered. "I can see if I had purple hair or something. . . ." "You don't realize how long you were on television," she was told. "You were on the cover of *Time*, *Newsweek*, *Sports Illustrated*, all in the same week. You're on our Wheaties box; you're *Seventeen*'s cover girl. . . ."

Her whole life had taken on a dream quality. The phone in Fairmont never stopped ringing. A couple of mail sacks arrived every day, some including marriage proposals, many addressed only to Mary Lou Retton, Olympic Champion.

It took her until Christmas, but she and her mother answered all of it, using a special postcard that had a picture of Mary Lou on the front. It was a small thing but if people took the trouble to write, Mary Lou felt they deserved an answer.

She went to Hollywood parties that included Linda Evans and

166

Tom Selleck, and was astonished to find herself at their center. Michael Jackson, one of her idols, said he was pleased to meet *her*.

"Here I'm dying because I'm meeting them, and they want to meet me," Mary Lou marveled. "It really makes you think that it's a crazy world."

Crazy and fun. She drove a red Corvette with MARY LOU license plates, lived in a high-rise Houston condo that overlooked a forest. She flew first-class to engagements across America, and giggled when flight attendants told curious coach passengers, no, they couldn't use the bathroom up front. Her life had changed unalterably, and Mary Lou had to figure out how she wanted to handle it. "You're set for life," people told her. "What are you going to do now?"

To begin with, there was unfinished academic business. Two more years of high school loomed, which she wanted to complete as soon as she could.

Once, she'd daydreamed about going to UCLA. Now, thanks to endorsement contracts, Mary Lou had enough money to pay her way for a hundred years. Exciting possibilities beckoned everywhere. She was still only sixteen.

Two years earlier she'd been terrified when television interviewers had come around. Now she felt relaxed and confident before a camera. Corporations wanted her not only for advertisements, but as a spokeswoman.

Before long she was flying off to business meetings and speaking to executives. Burt Reynolds called her, wanting to know if she would play a part in one of his movies. There were commercials to film, instructional cassettes to be recorded, and all of them offered the promise of more and different options down the road. All because Mary Lou had been in the perfect place at a moment that would never come again—and had made the most of it.

Karolyi had told her that months before they'd ever lit the flame inside the Coliseum. "To have the Olympic Games in your own country is such fantastic opportunity," he'd kept saying. "I would stand on my head and spit quarters for that chance."

The Games had been magic for Karolyi, too. Three years earlier he had walked Los Angeles streets as a pauper who spoke six languages, all of them useless. Now his Houston gymnasium had become the mecca of American gymnastics, *the* place you had to train if you wanted to be an Olympian.

In a matter of months his enrollment tripled, to fourteen hundred, with pupils from a dozen states and seven foreign countries. Every mother and her daughter, it seemed, wanted to sign up for Killer Gymnastics.

The building, which Karolyi had already expanded once, soon sprouted two new sections. A new quadrennium had begun, the goal Seoul in 1988, and within days Bela and Martha were back at work, instructing, correcting, exhorting.

After a few weeks Mary Lou was back there, too. The gym was her second home, the only place that still seemed normal to her. When eight-year-olds she'd trained alongside for months approached her meekly for her signature, Mary Lou was aghast.

"What do you *mean* autographs?" she said. "You *know* me."

Mary Lou wanted nothing to change there. Her body had tightened up within days after the Games, and she yearned for a Bela-style workout and some Bela-style wisecracks. He obliged her on both counts.

"Aha," he growled when she walked in the door. "So you decide to come back?" Martha grinned. "You *are* alive," she proclaimed.

Alive and itching for another challenge. Mary Lou had made history at Los Angeles but the next Olympics were half a world and a million years away. She wanted an obstacle to clear *now*.

The biggest obstacle, she realized, was herself. It was the Rocky Balboa syndrome. Could you win the world title, indulge yourself for months with banquets, interviews, endorsements, and a champion's trappings, and still find it in yourself to be hungry? Karolyi had quoted recent history that said you couldn't. No modern Olympic all-around champion had been worth a damn the following year. Not Turishcheva. Not Comaneci. Not Davidova. And they hadn't had a fraction of the temptations toward dissipation that Mary Lou had faced.

As 1984 became 1985, a natural goal loomed—an unprecedented third straight McDonald's American Cup women's title.

Rocky Balboa had been thumped when he ventured to defend his title without whittling his body into fighting trim and recapturing his desire. Mary Lou had seen *Rocky II*, and had taken it to heart.

"All the distractions and just not wanting to *do* it," she thought. "I can see that now. You do get spoiled. You go out and people treat you like a celebrity and you lose the hunger. You say, 'Hey, I don't want to go back to the gym and bruise myself and sweat and get all gross.' "

Karolyi had warned her that he could no longer stoke the hunger unless she wanted it stoked. "I will help you as much as I can," he said. "But you really have to want it. I can only push you so far."

The challenge appealed to her, just as the layout Tsukahara had once appealed to her. Turishcheva, Comaneci, and Davidova had considered the difficulty of returning to world-class form in a post-Olympic year, and had bagged it. The world had not heard from its newest Olympic champion, other than in street clothes, in months.

"The first thing they're going to look for," Mary Lou told herself, "is to see what kind of shape I'm in. To see whether I can get back into competitive form. I want to prove that I can."

You're taking such a big chance, her alter ego whispered. You have absolutely nothing to gain. So you win another American Cup. So what? Lose it, and . . . .

"And yet," Mary Lou decided, "you have to take chances."

So she went back to the gym in mid-January and put herself inside Bela's torture chamber. She burned off five months' worth of banquet and airline food, learned a new floor routine, and stretched herself like taffy on Martha's beam. "Guuud, guuud," Karolyi nodded.

And in early March Mary Lou went to Indianapolis for the American Cup, and put herself under the microscope. CBS was covering the event live. The international gymnastics federation had revised the scoring system since the Games, making 10s all but impossible. The Romanians, younger ones like Daniela Silivas and Camelia Voinea, were on hand. So were the Chinese.

"This is a beautiful Sunday afternoon," Mary Lou said to herself. "What are you doing this for?"

It was, she concluded, her obligation. You could not win an Olympic title and not give the world another shot at you. You owed it to yourself to be in top form. The competition would determine the rest.

What happened at Indianapolis was a string of 9.8s, the most consistent performance of Mary Lou's career. Everything was crisp and solid, and the beam—her nemesis—was the best of her life. China's Yu Feng, who placed second, was never a threat. Neither was Silivas, whom the Romanians were touting as the next Szabo.

So she'd made American Cup history, but the feeling was more relief than celebration. She'd survived the specter of *Rocky II*. "Whew!" Mary Lou thought. "I *did* it."

She had come full circle in only two years. In 1983 she had been a rising young gymnast, looking to make an international splash. In 1985 hundreds of millions of people knew her name, her face, and what she had accomplished on one Friday night in Los Angeles, when half (literally) of the world was watching.

Because of that the world had opened gates and offered her pathways that no Fairmont girl, no teenager anywhere, had ever seen. "It's like an all-American story," Mary Lou Retton would think months later. "Something you read about. Never, never did I dream it would happen to me. But it did."